# Spring Nature Activities for Children

Sov ial

-1 MAY 2012

D1428362

Imgard Kutsch and Brigitte Walden

# Spring Nature Activities for Children

Floris Books

Translated by Jane R. Helmchen

First published in German in 2001 as *Natur-Kinder-Garten-Werkstatt:*
*Frühling,* by Verlag Freies Geistesleben, Stuttgart
First published in English in 2005 by Rudolf Steiner College Press,
California and Floris Books, Edinburgh

Publication of this book has been made possible
by a grant from the Waldorf Curriculum Fund.

British Library CIP Data available

ISBN 0-86315-544-8

Produced in Poland by Polskabook

# Foreword

When you look at the environment in which our children live, you realize that many children these days only learn about nature from television or the internet. Many of them no longer have the opportunity to observe and experience nature first-hand. They live in virtual worlds where their heroes are pokemons and digimons. Often, they aren't taught about nature and the environment; indeed, you could argue that nature can't be taught, but rather must be experienced.

This series of Nature Activities for Children books hopes to address this situation. The aim is to give children the opportunity to (re)discover nature through play, and to experience nature first-hand and with all their senses. This is especially important for children who live in big cities, who may not come into contact with nature very often.

The books contain useful tips for teachers and parents who want to introduce children to the world of nature. I hope that they will work to:

✿ fill our children with a love of, and respect for, nature; and
✿ give them the chance to grow and develop in a natural environment.

Children are especially open to, and ready for, new experiences.

In my opinion, an upbringing which gives children this kind of knowledge and experience is an essential foundation for life lived in harmony with nature. Before children absorb the consumer ideals of our society, we need to guide them towards responsible, forward-looking lifestyles with an emphasis on sustainability and living well rather than wanting more.

For this reason, I wish all of the readers of these books much inspiration and insight.

*Bärbel Höhn, Minister for the Environment and Protection of Nature, Germany*

# The Story of this Book

## Supporting children's interest in the world

This is Lea-Marie. She is a year and a half old and, like all children of this age, loves to approach her world directly and very imaginatively. She wants to touch everything, all the time, and, through touching, understand her world. What options does she have in the top picture, and what does she have in the bottom picture? How would her sense of balance and her ability to move around develop in each case, if she only stayed in one or the other? What opportunities for playing would she have? What stimulation would her senses receive, her eyes, nose, ears, hands? Let's not leave out her sense of taste, too; Lea-Marie has often "tasted" sand and decided it tasted awful. That, too, is an important sensing experience.

Her parents understand the importance of a natural environment full of life for children. They have dressed Lea-Marie in "garden trousers" and sturdy shoes and let her play, experiment, and move about as often and for as long as possible; they just let her be. Lea-Marie can rattle, mash and throw sand, stones, water and clay, surrounded by fragrant plants. It is obvious what an invigorating and, at the same time, quieting influence a natural environment has on children and how it helps to train their concentration.

8

## Promoting children's health

What was just described is one of many situations that remind me how important life in and with nature is for child development. I saw this especially in my work with children with developmental disabilities in special schools and in kindergartens.

Being outside in a natural environment encourages harmony. In addition, in nature there are lots of opportunities for children to develop meaningful relationships with their world, which can give them direction later in life.

Children who have been able to touch the world have, for example, a much better chance of being able to learn through electronic media. The computer is not, of course, a substitute for life experiences. Being in contact with nature is a prerequisite for computer-based education and an ability to communicate.

To make the world *touchable* — that is, *livable* through all your senses and therefore *understandable* — is essential in an age when children's social and ecological frameworks are changing radically — and unfortunately seldom for the good of the children.

## Founding the Children's Nature and Garden Centre in Reichshof, Germany

In 1994, I was a nature teacher connected to the Steiner-Waldorf schools movement. At that time, I had several key experiences which left me with the following questions:

✿ How can children experience a traditional life, as it was meant to be?

✿ How can children relate meaningfully to life in as many ways as possible?

✿ How can awareness of nature and environmental protection be developed at an early age, so that children become responsible adults?

✿ How can parents, teachers and others cross the generation gap to meet and work with children as equals?

✿ How can nature teaching for children be integrated into local, cultural and historical frameworks, to encourage intercultural experiences?

✿ How can work with nature help to prevent drug use?

✿ How can schools and kindergartens become more than just economically-based services, and be developed into more humane environments?

✿ How can discussions about standards be switched from quantitative to qualitative grounds?

✿ Will there be an increased understanding that a child is a unique individual with a right to personal development?

✿ Can the professional image of the teacher develop into the idea of teachers as companions, oriented to the needs of the child?

❀ Can the Children's Nature and Garden Centre play a role within the global ecological movement?

Some of these questions have found preliminary answers in the course of time and in the development of this book. Most of them, however, are ongoing and call for continuing exchange of ideas among colleagues and reflection on current affairs.

## Who is this book for?

This book is one of a series of four looking at the different seasons of the year. It is intended to encourage cooperation between professionals in different areas, to promote the well-being of children and of nature, and thus the future of our world.

All four books are written primarily for teachers in kindergartens, child centres, children's homes, primary schools and special-needs schools. It doesn't matter whether a school is introducing a new curriculum or whether an individual teacher wants to do more nature-based activities. The important thing is to give children exposure to traditional methods, and within this, any philosophical approach — such as Steiner-Waldorf or Montessori — can work.

These books can also be used in continuing education for teachers, as well as by families, young people, old people, community administrators and politicians. People from all walks of life have contributed to these books.

They offer situation-based and experience-based options for nature teaching. When writing the books, we have consciously avoided discussing teaching theory; there are plenty of other books on the market that do this.

We hope that these books will bring together open-minded people who are looking for a new direction, with help and ideas from many sources. We hope that the books will be a bridge between people with something to give and those with something to learn for the sake of a human- and nature-centred future.

## How does this series of books work?

These books developed out of the everyday practice of the Children's Nature and Garden Centre in Reichshof. Its practical, sense-oriented workshops travel to kindergartens far and wide and projects normally last for several days, with children, parents, teachers and others all involved. We also work with adult education and consult on the development of natural playgrounds for children.

Each book sets out a series of monthly themes based on nature and the season, with suggestions for practical work with children. From countless options available, we have chosen those projects that best stimulate the senses, and which promote a new understanding of everyday objects and the world around us. We protect what we love!

The garden and handicraft activities are intended primarily for teachers who work with children between the ages of five and ten. In mixed-age kindergarten groups, the youngest children tend to be busy exploring materials in an unfocused, but very imaginative, way. Older children look for ways to do "real" work. Both unfocused play and movement, and purposeful work, offer possibilities for developing practical intelligence, which is especially important in primary and special-needs schools. The key is to always have an appropriately-busy adult for the children to imitate.

When choosing the content of these books, we have always kept in mind the child as a whole personality, in a particular phase of mental, emotional and physical development. All of the topics discussed have been selected with an eye to creating — with as little specialized knowledge as possible and with minimum expense — a natural environment rich in sense experience and full of life for the child's development. This is illustrated by many colorful photos and drawings that come almost entirely from the work of the Children's Nature and Garden Centre.

The particular themes need not be tied to specific months of the year. This is only intended as a guide for those who do not yet have a close enough connection with nature to be confident in their timing. In addition, each individual topic can stand alone when planning lessons for an introduction to the cycles of nature. If some activities are repeated in the course of a year, the children will feel grounded in the natural surroundings.

The side-bars throughout the book have been contributed by different people who have participated in projects at the Children's Nature and Garden Centre. They can suggest ways of collaborating with different individuals and organizations; institutions for children need a protective, supporting circle of friends.

*Irmgard Kutsch*

# Between Heaven and Earth

## The course of the year and its relationship to the cosmos

Have you heard children ask questions such as:

- ❀ How do apples get onto the trees?
- ❀ Why are the leaves coloured?
- ❀ Where do butterflies go in wintertime?
- ❀ Where does the sun sleep?
- ❀ Why don't the stars fall out of the sky?

Child-like amazement and natural curiosity can awaken us to the phenomena of the world. As adult companions, we have to give children the opportunity to gather knowledge that they can understand about heaven and earth. As small children, we too had instincts about how things worked and why things happened, and we wanted to find out more. We developed questions, like those above, which allowed us to collect knowledge.

Adults should not answer children's questions with too much detail, since this upsets their natural wonder at the phenomenon, and lessens their observation. A small child might see the first germinating acorn in a flower pot and be amazed and delighted that "the little tree is growing." The intellectual adult might describe this phenomenon as "early germination."

We mustn't forget, though, that adults too have questions about the relationship of human beings to the world around us: are we just born into geographic, social and cultural-historical relationships, or are there also powers, rhythms and arrangements behind these that influence us just as strongly?

These questions have been around for thousands of years. Our distant ancestors, although not gifted with highly intellectual powers of understanding, realized intuitively that their planet not only obeyed its own laws, but was part of a tremendous organism — space — whose parts move in constant relationship to each other. In their imaginative consciousness, they saw the sun and stars as a "sun wagon" that passed by the zodiac symbols in the sky. The sun was also seen as the power that turned the wheel of life and influenced the seasons of the year.

In this way, our ancestors experienced the life-giving changes of day and night. They even gave names to the days of the week in relation to the planets. The course of the moon was used as a time line for a month. Through observation and experience, they recognized the rhythm of the consecutive seasons with their individual characteristics.

Each constellation of the planetary system was seen as being connected with nature. Up to about 100 years ago, a farmer who wanted to sow his grain was able to determine the right moment by the position of the sun and the moon in the sky.

Even today, we can't imagine life without these time rhythms — at least without serious health implications. If the rhythm is broken, the person is broken. The feeling of being part of these structures and powers creates a deep confidence, a reliable base for everything that we want to do. This is apparent in the drawing by the seven-year-old on the opposite page.

Let's now go on a small journey of discovery into the world of cosmic rhythms, so that we can learn to read nature's calendar, and plan and carry out the right thing at the right time.

Imagine the sky as a beautiful festive ballroom that is decorated with twelve zodiac symbols. In the inner room, the dancers have been turning in orderly harmony since the beginning of time. The sun determines the way they move - their rhythm and tempo. Around them, Saturn, Jupiter, Mars, Venus, Mercury and the moon are dancing in a circle (see figure, p. 15). Our ancestors were so closely bound to this dance in heaven that they not only aligned this heavenly relationship to nature and their farming methods, but also reflected this image in their earthly lives as an example of harmonious social communication. Among other things, they developed a lively, happy form of community activity: the folk dance.

Eventually someone developed the clock with its twelve-part face as a reflection of the cosmos. To give primary-school children a feeling for time, give them a clock with a face and hands. Only after they have a sense of the heavenly-time arrangement should we give them a digital clock, which only shows the precise moment without demonstrating the relationships of time.

Just as our ancestors did, we can participate today in the grand dance of the cosmos every year. Led by the sun, we watch the planets move from one zodiac sign to the next: the Moon, Mercury and Venus dance about one month in front of each zodiac sign, while Mars, Jupiter and Saturn move in a stately manner through the heavens. The Sun moves with its companions through the entire course of the twelve zodiac signs in one year. The nature calendar resulting from this is the basis for the diagram on page 16, which shows the "becoming," "being" and "dying" of the plant-world's annual rhythm.

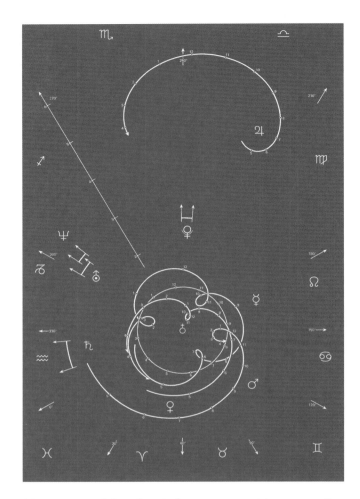

*Movements of the planets from a geocentric perspective*

Human beings have carried out specific tasks according to the position of the sun since the beginning of time: in spring they sow seeds; in summer they care for the plants; in autumn they harvest the plants so that in winter they will have a supply of what they need to live.

Out of respect for cosmic influences on the natural events of our world, we have chosen several thematic areas that can help orient small

PLANISPHÆRIVM Sive VNIVERSI TO EX HYPO COPERNI PLANO

COPERNICANVM Systema TIVS CREATI THESI CANA IN EXHIBITVM

children in time and space during the course of a year, so as to feel at home on planet Earth. Our calendar year begins with January. However, as we are following European seasonal events from spring, through summer and autumn to winter, we will begin with the spring month of March.

*The zodiac circle is like a ballroom with twelve signs around the perimeter, and our planetary system is like a well-ordered formation of dancers. This representation comes from the heavenly atlas of Cellarius in 1661. It shows the world from the viewpoint of Copernicus.*

15

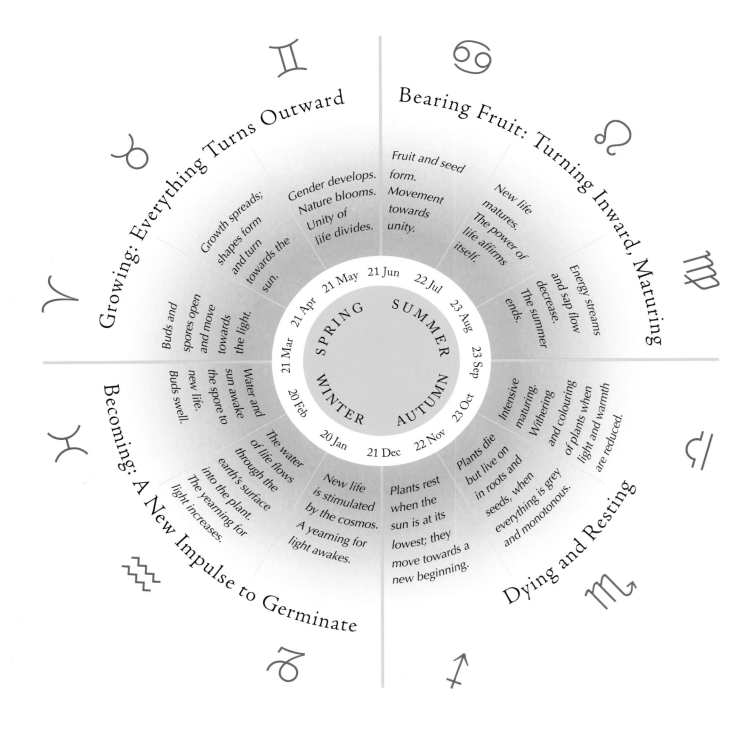

Growing: Everything Turns Outward

Bearing Fruit: Turning Inward, Maturing

Dying and Resting

Becoming: A New Impulse to Germinate

Growth spreads; shapes form and turn towards the sun.

Gender develops. Nature blooms. Unity of life divides.

Fruit and seed form. Movement towards unity.

New life matures. The power of life affirms itself.

Energy streams and sap flow decrease. The summer ends.

Buds and spores open and move towards the light. Buds swell.

Water and sun awake the spore to new life.

Intensive maturing. Withering and colouring of plants when light and warmth are reduced.

The water of life flows through the earth's surface into the plant. The yearning for light increases.

New life is stimulated by the cosmos. A yearning for light awakes.

Plants rest when the sun is at its lowest; they move towards a new beginning.

Plants die but live on in roots and seeds, when everything is grey and monotonous.

SPRING
SUMMER
WINTER
AUTUMN

21 Mar
21 Apr
21 May
21 Jun
22 Jul
23 Aug
23 Sep
23 Oct
22 Nov
21 Dec
20 Jan
20 Feb

*OPPOSITE: The course of the year*

# March

Nesting

Sowing, sprouting, growing

As human beings, we are bound to the seasonal changes of nature with rhythms determined by the cosmos. Through the course of the twentieth century, the knowledge of how people and nature influence each other — and even how individual areas of nature need each other — has been forgotten or lost. However, more and more people are beginning to take a renewed interest in annual rhythms. Those who work with children should encourage this interest as much as possible.

Events in the plant world at the end of February and the beginning of March are reflected in the zodiac sign of Pisces, the fish ()-(): dying life remains behind; new life breaks out. Spring arrives in giant leaps: invisible to us, roots and spores underground, which have taken in the water of life and been saturated by the sun, can now be awakened to new life.

The zodiac sign of Aries, the ram (♈) has thrusting horns. Anyone familiar with this animal can see why our ancestors chose this symbol for the season when the plant world breaks out and breaks through — the power of germination bursting their seeds and working through the earth. Above the ground, leaf and blossom buds are clearly swelling. Protected from the cold night air by strong covering leaves, they are waiting — tightly rolled or folded — for the warming sun of spring.

The first birds arrive back from the south. Now, the hedges, bushes, trees, fields, forests and meadows become nurseries. March rabbits are born. The birds find their mates, look for a place to live, build their nests and lay eggs. The bees, after their winter rest, start collecting catkin and hazelnut pollen. The squirrels look for deserted nests to live in. The hedgehog leaves its winter home and starts looking for earthworms and early snails. The nuts and acorns left behind start to grow in unexpected spots in the garden.

Thoughtless use of nature's gifts has led to an imbalance in the changing relationships of nature. In many areas, human treatment of living things has made nature sick, or even destroyed it. Alarm signals that cannot be overlooked, such as dying forests or the extreme flooding of recent years, warn us to rethink the situation and to act soon.

To change life and behaviour patterns and priorities, the best place to start is in preschool teaching and during the first years of school.

The absolute prerequisite for this, however, is a positive learning situation for the child in kindergartens and schools. Class sizes, the number of staff, the number of rooms and funding must all be radically improved. Teachers need continuing education. Couples also need further education to prepare them to be parents.

Right from the beginning, children need an insight into basic natural relationships from which an active feeling of responsibility for nature can

grow. The thoughts, feelings and will of every child should be encouraged to keep them in tune with nature.

How can children learn to form living relationships as early as pre-school? The answer is by imitating an adult or older siblings. Role models are extremely important, especially in the area of environmental education. Small children develop their approach to everyday objects, to activities, and to their entire environment, through how the adults around them behave.

For this reason, the main goal of this book is to look again and again at natural relationships from various viewpoints, and through this to give direction and support to the adults who act as companions and role models to children.

# Nesting

## Our Native Birds in Spring

How deeply moved we are by the blackbird's first spring song — first very soft, then stronger every day. Children can easily recognize these black birds with a yellow bill by both their appearance and their song.

More than 160 kinds of birds live in our part of the world, and each contributes its own melody to the dawn chorus. "I'm here," calls one bird and invites another to join him. "Come on, let's build a nest!" The mother bird lays her eggs in the nest and sits on them. In some species, partners take turns at looking after the eggs.

The blackbird's nest looks like half a coconut. The finches build a wonderfully soft cradle of moss, spiders' webs, hair and wool. Blue tits like to decorate their nests with wool, colourful threads and feathers. They all do this the same way every year, so it's easy to recognize what kind of bird has built the nest.

Birds that nest openly in trees, hedges, meadows and fields are called "branch nesters" or "ground nesters." These include blackbirds, wrens, warblers and many others, including the cuckoo except that this bird lays its eggs in others' nests and has the other birds hatch the egg and raise the young bird.

"Hole nesters" include tits, starlings, flycatchers, woodpeckers and others that look for nesting possibilities in high trees, which are becoming harder to find as forests are gradually felled. For this reason, these birds like to use nesting boxes that people prepare for them. This is a good place for children to observe how often the parent birds have to come

*What fun! The finished nesting boxes are ready to be put up. There is also a box for bats.* ➤

and go in order to find enough food for the young birds, and how the baby birds begin to fly.

"Eave nesters" and "platform nesters" include wagtails, robins and others that like to build their nests under roofs, in holes in the wall, in sheds or even in old garden shoes, pots and mailboxes. Some of these birds, especially sparrows, are very industrious pest eaters. However, in nature there is no good or bad, just as there is basically no useful or harmful. Everything is in harmony with everything else — if humans didn't mess things up. We too are bound into the circle of creation and are only a tiny link in the chain of events.

If we remember this, our feathered friends will continue to sing to us every spring — and we will join in with them.

*Ruth Hecht, forester*

*A nesting box begins with a round piece of wood, a mallet and a chisel* ▼

## Even Younger Children Can Help Build a Nesting Box

This project is suitable for children from the age of three upwards. Adults should first prepare stencils for the floor, roof and side walls of the nesting box to the right size. Younger workers can then place the stencils onto the wood, and copy the patterns onto the wood. Remember that accurate measurements with a ruler can be difficult for children under ten. Sawing must be supervised by an adult. Be careful never to use blunt saws: the danger of injury is too great, and the lack of success is discouraging. Three- to four-year-olds can then sand the edges of the pieces of wood until they are smooth as silk. They like this task even more if the sandpaper is wrapped around a small block that they can grasp with their small hands.

When the wood pieces are ready to be put together, it is a good idea to drill the holes for the nails in advance, because this makes nailing much easier for the children.

# Nesting Help for Birds

## — Box for hole nesters

Hole-nesting birds have more and more difficulty finding natural nesting places in our cities and gardens. We can help by providing simple nesting boxes. In order not to favour a particular kind of bird, different boxes — or at least boxes with different sized entrance holes — should be built.

MATERIALS
* ❀ well-dried unfinished pinewood
* ❀ nails and two wood screws or a hook bent like a figure 8 (from a wire clothes hanger)

MEASUREMENTS
* ❀ 56 × 7" (140.5 × 18cm), wood thickness: 1" (2.4cm)

INSTRUCTIONS

The measurements given should only be used with wood that is 1" (2.4cm) thick. Different thicknesses would need different measurements. Assemble the pieces in the following order: 1, 2, 3, 5, 6, 4.

The upper edge of the back wall should be slanted below the roof so that there is no gap between the wall and the roof. The opening swing mechanism is made with two nails placed at the same height and hammered from the side walls into the front wall (marked *FW* in diagram). Two more nails should be bent to use as a fastening (marked *N* in diagram).

HANGING THE NESTING BOX

Hole nester boxes should be placed facing south-east, about 6–13 feet (2–4m) off the ground.

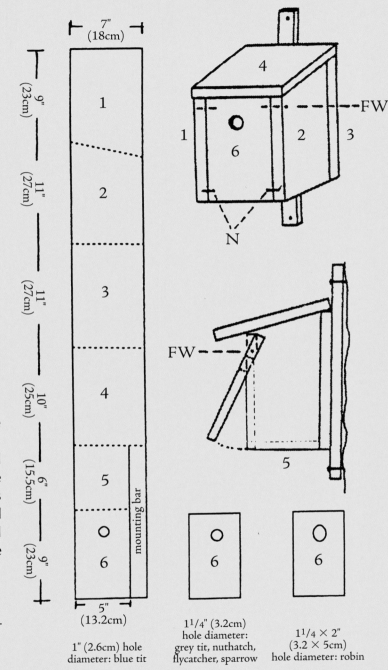

1" (2.6cm) hole diameter: blue tit

1¹/₄" (3.2cm) hole diameter: grey tit, nuthatch, flycatcher, sparrow

1¹/₄ × 2" (3.2 × 5cm) hole diameter: robin

23

# — Box for eave or platform nesters

### MATERIALS
* well-dried unfinished pinewood
* wood thickness: 1" (2.4cm)
* board or hook for hanging up the nesting box

### MEASUREMENTS
* $38^{1/2} \times 6"$ (98.2 × 16cm)

### INSTRUCTIONS

The measurements given are only for use with wood that is 1" (2.4cm) thick. Otherwise, the floor will need to be a different size. (Note that nominally 1" thick lumber is actually $^{3/4}$" after drying. This standard size is assumed for the project. You should check the fit of pieces before gluing.)

Assemble the pieces in the following order: 1, 2, 3, 4, 5, 6.

### WATERPROOFING

Waterproofing is usually not necessary because the boxes dry quickly after rain and last several years even without treatment. Do not use commercial wood sealing products, because they give off poisonous fumes. A covering of tar paper can cause dampness from condensation.

### HANGING THE NESTING BOX

Eave nester boxes can be placed on a building, possibly under a roof. Boxes should be placed only in areas where no plant or insect pesticides are used where the birds will look for food. Otherwise the birds will gather poisoned food and may become seriously ill or die. All baby birds need protein-rich nourishment; with poisoned food, the whole brood could be lost.

In their natural search for food, birds keep so-called pests under control. Don't feed them bread, cake crumbs, etc. It is much better to create places for them to live with enough natural nourishment.

### CLEANING

After every brood, remove the old nests and clean the nesting box with a brush and soapy water. If the nesting box has become occupied by hornets or bumblebees, don't disturb them and clean only after they've left. These creatures also need nesting places. Dormice sometimes hibernate in nesting boxes; wait until they leave in spring and then clean.

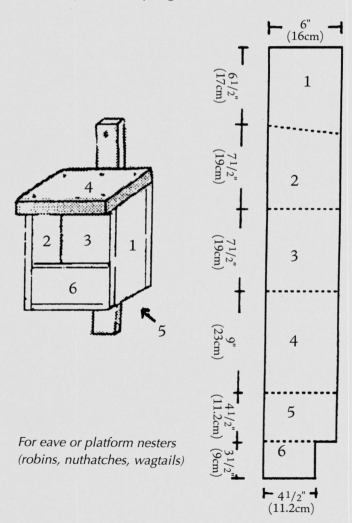

For eave or platform nesters
(robins, nuthatches, wagtails)

# Sowing, sprouting, growing

## Sprouting Grain

Germinating grain demonstrates especially clearly the spring process of renewal after death. It reflects the death and resurrection themes of Easter; throughout the year, in fact, connections between nature and different religions, not just Christianity, can be discussed. Sprouting grain is a very positive image for children in our battered world; the children themselves are also growing, so sowing and caring for grain, then watching the germinating power of the seed cause it to grow, is especially relevant for them.

During germination, the young plants grow 1–2" (3–5cm) per day. Use clay pots or bowls, homemade if possible. Fill them with earth, ideally with fresh garden compost; sow the seeds; and cover them with a thin layer of finely sieved earth. The imagery is of returning the seeds to the earth as if putting them in a grave, only for them to live again.

These bowls are sometimes called Easter bowls. If our Easter bowls are placed in a light, warm spot, and if we water them well but not too well, the first shoots will appear after five to ten days. After this, they grow several centimetres per day and you can almost hear them growing. The bowls should be covered overnight with a light foil so that they don't dry out. Over Easter, the children can take the bowls home to care for them. Easter bowls are especially nice when they

are decorated with a twig, a red ribbon and a golden egg. A small rooster made of yeast dough can sit on top of the decoration. It's also nice to hide a small rabbit in the soil.

The *red ribbon* is a symbol of love, joy and the resurrection at Easter.

The *golden egg* is an ancient symbol from many creation myths about the appearance of the Earth, the heavens and the sun. The egg is also the origin of hope and new life. For Germanic tribes, it was the symbol of fertility. For Christians it is a symbol of resurrection.

The *rabbit* symbolizes selfless love. In nature it is known to sacrifice itself for another rabbit in trouble or being hunted. Its long ears and alert eyes represent its awareness of its environment. In

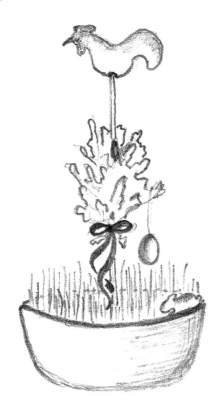

ancient myths, the rabbit was a symbol for fertility.

If teachers understand the meanings of these age-old symbols, the children will absorb the ideas subconsciously by imitation. In this way they will better understand their culture's customs and their connection to beliefs and seasonal events.

When children create festive decorations, their aesthetic sensitivity is exercised. Through repeated exposure, they will develop a feeling for the qualities of different materials and for what feels "right." It's important, therefore, to use mainly natural materials in kindergarten and primary school, because these support the development of the senses.

After Easter, the children should bring their Easter bowls back to kindergarten or school. When the first grass is high enough to bend over, it should be planted in the garden and cared for until it is mature and can be observed. This is a straightforward way to reinforce children's understanding that grain is the source of basic human food, even in our fast-food world. In August you can harvest and work with grain you have planted yourself (see the *Summer* book in this series).

# Caring for Flowers

▲ He is holding a secret piece of "pure nature" in his hands. The grown-ups say, "It is alive . . ." ➤

"It needs earth, water, air and warmth to grow and develop. Maybe this secret something will even have beautiful colourful flowers and long green leaves," they say. ▼

▲ Hyacinth bulbs are happy with only one glass of water when they develop in warmth and light. The water should only be as high as the top of the root. Children can easily observe the growth of the roots, leaves and flowers.

## Sprouting Walnuts

Even a windowsill can hold an impressive nature experience — such as sprouting walnuts.

Children's senses can be stimulated just by putting nuts in glasses with water, and placing them on the windowsill. The nuts need fresh water every day, so that they don't rot. The nuts, which have dried out over the winter, soak up enough water to double their original weight; they become fat and heavy. Eventually they split open and — surprise! — the shoot peeps out.

They should then be planted carefully in flower pots with soil, so that the shoots stick out above the earth. Cover everything with damp leaves and take care that the new plant doesn't dry out. Children like to spray the surface of the soil with water from a spray bottle. In addition, you could cover the pot with clear plastic foil, but this should be removed from time to time so that mould and rot don't develop (in any case, the shoots need air).

It is essential, when working with living things, to give them regular, reliable care. If we take a living creature out of its natural surroundings to observe it, then we are responsible for its continuing existence. It is important to emphasise this principle to children: to value living things and developing life.

The best time to plant the seed in children for the correct care of plants and animals is when they are very young. For children this is hands-on bioethics in the truest sense.

You can carefully lift the leaves of a tree to see the developing shoots. The bud shapes are magical wonders of nature, and can't be admired enough!

*The walnut powerfully pushes the root out of its shell and sinks it into the dark, damp soil*

*Then the first shoot unfolds its leaves, reaching toward the light*

When, after weeks of loving, observant care in the "tree nursery" the young plants are strong enough, replant them in their proper natural surroundings. It is wonderful if one or more of the little trees can stay in the kindergarten or schoolyard. Otherwise, give them to friends or relatives for their gardens or they can find a spot in a school garden. Perhaps they can be given away at a school fête in return for a small contribution. Alternatively, see if you can take a field trip and, after consultation with the proper authorities, plant the little trees at the edge of a wood. In any case, it is good to be able to continue to watch them grow. We have a responsibility to make sure that all the plants we grow are well cared for.

From now on, during spring walks in the woods, the children will discover the shoots of different woodland trees and also of other plants; and they will want us to share in their delight in all that they discover.

In order to give children even stronger emotional feelings about tree-planting, they can be told the story of Johnny Appleseed (see page 30). The figures on pages 32 and 33 can be traced, cut out and used for shadow puppet performances of the story. We recommend that the story should be *told* — not read aloud — every day for a week. During the second week, the story should be performed as shadow or puppet theatre by the adults. During the third week, the older children can do this for the younger ones. Experience shows that children often ask to hear a story for more than three weeks in order to take it in deeply. There are also songs that can be sung.

## Johnny Appleseed Grace

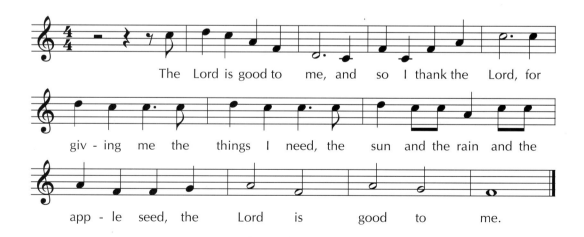

The Lord is good to me, and so I thank the Lord, for giv-ing me the things I need, the sun and the rain and the app-le seed, the Lord is good to me.

## Johnny Appleseed

*American folk story based on the life of John Chapman 1774–1845.*

Once upon a time there was a boy called Johnny. He grew up in Massachusetts, in America, with his father and mother and eleven brothers and sisters. With such a large family, they needed to grow a lot of food. Johnny loved working in the garden — and he especially loved apples. He felt his family was particularly blessed to have apple trees that gave them baskets and baskets of delicious fruit. Every day they thanked God for this blessing.

When he was young, Johnny asked his mother where the apple trees came from. His mother showed him how, inside each apple, there are little brown seeds growing in little star-shaped houses. She said, "If you plant a seed in the earth, and if it has enough sunshine and rain, it will have — with God's blessing — everything it needs to grow into a big apple tree."

When Johnny became a young man, he wanted to leave his home and see the world, as many young men do. He also wanted to take his delicious apples to people who did not have any. Johnny said, "Mother, please give me a big sack of apples and a cooking pot, so I can travel west." His mother was sad to see her tall, strong son leave, but he was now a man, and she did as he asked.

Johnny picked up the heavy sack of apples and lifted it onto his shoulder. With such a heavy load, he couldn't also carry the cooking pot, so he wore it on his head like a hat!

After a few hours of walking, Johnny felt tired and hungry. He put down his great sack and sat down in the shade to eat two or three apples, carefully saving the seeds to plant later. Then he continued his journey until, near sunset, he came to a farmhouse. The family there welcomed him and gave him supper and a place to sleep for the night. To thank them for their kindness, he planted an orchard of apple trees with the seeds of the apples he had eaten for lunch the day before. And he thanked God and asked him to send sun and rain to make the new apple trees grow.

Johnny continued on his way. He walked for many days, and months, and years. He met many more people, and he planted many, many, many apple trees. In each place, he asked people to take good care of the trees and to thank God for his blessings.

Johnny became famous for this work. People remembered the tall, strong, kind man with the cooking-pot hat. They didn't always remember his whole name, but they knew he always planted apple trees, so they just called him Johnny Appleseed.

When Johnny traveled back to his home many years later, he saw orchard after orchard of apple trees that he had planted. He traveled through many American states: Pennsylvania, Ohio, Kentucky, Illinois and Indiana. This happened more than 150 years ago, and some of the trees he planted are still bearing delicious apples today.

*It's a miracle that big maple trees can grow from these tiny shoots*

A seed hidden in the heart of an apple is an orchard invisible.

*Welsh Proverb*

And this, our life, exempt from public haunt, finds tongues in trees, books in the running brooks, sermons in stones, and good in everything.

*William Shakespeare*

The kingdom of heaven is like a mustard-seed, which a man took and sowed in his field. As a seed, mustard is smaller than any other; but when it has grown it is bigger than any garden plant; it becomes a tree, big enough for the birds to come and dwell among its branches.

*Matthew 13.33*

I think that I shall never see
A poem lovely as a tree.
A tree whose hungry mouth is prest
Against the earth's sweet flowing breast;
A tree that looks at God all day
And lifts her leafy arms to pray;
A tree that may in Summer wear
A nest of robins in her hair;
Upon whose bosom snow has lain;
Who intimately lives with rain.
Poems are made by fools like me,
But only God can make a tree.

*Joyce Kilmer*

We all travel the milky way together, trees and men ... trees are travellers, in the ordinary sense. They make journeys, not very extensive ones, it is true: but our own little comes and goes are only little more than tree-wavings — many of them not so much.

*John Muir*

# April

## Creating garden spaces

# Garden Work and Health

Discussion of the healing effects of gardens and plants has been almost entirely limited to the valuable substances to be found in plants. The effects on healthy and sick human beings of garden work have only been investigated by environmental psychologists and horticultural therapists. There are very few empirical studies in the existing literature.

Plants have a strong will to survive, and an outstanding ability to adapt and heal themselves. Plants have been known to produce whatever they need to survive: unusual roots; substitute parts; even getting oxygen from water condensation on roots.

Everything plants produce — including their shape and colour — inspires people. The garden allows us to think back to our roots and past. Gardens are often described as places of recognition, in which we can perceive, feel, consider and develop.

Gardens create emotional experiences by providing access to the life and development of the plants. Most people can make the connection between the life of the plants and their own lives. Some people compare the ups and downs of their own life stories with the rhythms in nature.

Both quietness and liveliness in gardens influence people. Human beings' physical and emotional powers are stimulated and strengthened by being in a garden. Harmony and vitality are increased, and aggression and longing can be constructively channelled.

Gardens are nourishment for our life forces. They connect us to the process of life, through touch and movement, and through the opportunity to personally shape part of the environment.

*Konrad Neuberger, teacher and gardener*

"When the world seems to tremble, a glance at a flower can restore balance."

*Ernst Jünger*

At the beginning of April, vegetation is still being influenced by the zodiac sign of Aries, the ram (♈) with its thrusting power. But the plant world slowly begins to develop more leaves under the sign of Taurus, the bull (♉). This can be related to the fact that the cow or bull eats as much as it wants and transforms the food by chewing and ruminating it in a complicated process, until it becomes energy and strength, and also fertile manure. A particular achievement of the animal's metabolism is the transformation of an enormous amount of food into the cow's fragrant, life-giving milk.

In April, the snow has melted, frost and dampness leave the ground, and plants sprout with strength and vitality. Everything is pointed toward light, leaving darkness behind.

A mysterious power develops in the plant world: shoots and buds burst their seeds and push toward sunlight. Everything is focused on growth. By now, the bees are finding enough nourishment from spring flowers. We have to be considerate not to disturb baby birds in their nests.

Garden tasks are most intensive in April. Working the earth in the fresh air, observing growth, enjoying the weather and the pleasure of success from physical labour all have a healthy effect on the body, soul and spirit of young and old alike.

*Seeds harvested at the end of summer are now placed in the ground* ➤

# Landscaping a Garden as a Group Project

## ~ Actively shaping our surroundings

Our modern industrial society is slowly moving away from thinking that encourages control and exploitation of nature for short-term profit, and is beginning instead to search, with an increased feeling of responsibility, for new paths towards global balance. Everywhere in our society, you can sense a new beginning that promises great potential for action. There are lots of opportunities for cooperation between government agencies and individuals, health insurance companies, nature and environmental protection organizations, industry and crafts, art and commerce, politics and education, and many others.

*Agenda 21* is the action plan for the benefit of the world's people and ecosystems that was passed at the environmental summit in Rio de Janeiro in June 1992, and was signed by the leaders of more than 170 developing and industrial countries. Based on the official statement, "Think globally — act locally," environmental protection is to be combined with social, cultural and economic development, while considering local needs. Now is the time for action. We are called upon to shape our surroundings actively, together with other interested and capable people, and to help our environment to become something unique, beautiful and natural — or, perhaps, to help it return to this state.

It doesn't matter whether this involves taking the concrete out of a schoolyard, taking over a public park, working together to landscape some available land with several families, returning a brook to its natural state, or reshaping the grounds around a kindergarten: personal initiative is called for and will be supported.

The action guidelines of *Agenda 21* can, of course, be included in the educational objectives of a kindergarten or a school. We should ask ourselves:

* How can a kindergarten be an ark in which plants, animals and humans all have their place?

* How can schools run ecological workshops to build a better future?

* How can big city kindergartens and schools become part of a network of ecosystems, where many people can create social, eco-logically-sound environments?

* How can these ecosystem "islands" be at least partially connected by fences and hedges acting as paths for our two-, four-, six-, and eight-legged friends (see p. 44)?

## ⚊ Gardens at the root of social change

How many elderly people are there in our immediate neighborhood who, since retiring, see no more purpose to life? How many single parents live among us in total isolation? How many young people around us get into trouble because no one has shown them the point of living?

One option is to create a garden work group with people looking for practical leisure activities and who have a real interest in living together in harmony with nature. Above and beyond over-

worked teachers and working parents, kindergartens and schools need a circle of people who will help care for the school garden responsibly, especially if the garden is large and is a teaching garden. Just think of weekends and holiday times. Nothing is more frustrating (and irresponsible) than coming back after a holiday to a completely dried out and weed-filled garden that had, up until then, been cared for with much love and effort.

It goes without saying that people from outside the school who take on the responsibility of being regular garden assistants must receive recognition for their work and should be included, somehow, in the life of the community. They could, for example, be invited to parties, receive part of the harvest, or have their birthdays celebrated. In this way, give-and-take can be brought into a healthy balance, as it should be in every human group.

Here are some examples of how people might work together.

In the town of Siegen in Germany, an environment agency offered to work with kindergartens and schools. The young men who, instead of doing military service, were doing an alternative social service, were put to work developing the kindergarten's grounds into natural, friendly places. Gardeners and people from the environment agency had some good ideas for the teachers as to how the grounds could be landscaped and used for working with children and parents. In addition, the environment agency erected small greenhouses and paid for the materials for the beds and paths, and garden tools.

The town of Neuss worked with a sports academy in Cologne, the police, health insurance companies and volunteer nature and environmental protection organizations to organize an information exchange event for teachers about creating outdoor nature areas appropriate for children. They had an excellent response and many topics were considered through discussion circles, lectures and information booths.

One organization showed how an asphalt desert in the middle of the city could be turned into a green, blooming living space through the initiative of the students themselves. Because of increasing traffic, resulting in a need for more roads, there are fewer and fewer play areas for children, especially in the big cities. It is essential that children play and are imaginatively active, and become familiar with nature. One result of removing the large areas of concrete was that the tendency towards fighting among children during breaktime disappeared almost completely.

In the small and idyllic village of Wiehl, the local council and others were looking for new ways to landscape a park. At the same time, various interest groups approached the town, looking to be involved in *Agenda 21* work. These included a senior group that wanted to work together with younger people. Student initiatives at various school levels and a community-supported youth centre wanted to work for the environment and had already taken part in competitions for, for example, saving energy.

The Children's Nature and Garden Centre was asked to present a proposal for how best to proceed. The proposal combined work by young people and old people, and included recommendations for the integration of immigrant communities, courses for amateur gardeners, activities for the unemployed, and continuing education for teachers. It was very well-received, and straight after the meeting, a local bank called to offer financial support for the forward-looking project.

# What to Consider When Landscaping a Garden

## – Initial considerations

The following considerations should be taken into account before beginning to landscape a new garden area. The working group should first consider the surrounding countryside:

❀ How does the area fit into the surrounding land and what borders directly on the area?
   For example, a residential area, streets, industry, railway tracks, water, forests, fields etc.

❀ What kind of living relationships result from these neighbouring areas?
   *Plant communities:* flowering plants, trees and shrubs
   *Animal communities:* insects, birds, reptiles mammals (ask a biologist to survey the area)

❀ What are the characteristics of the surrounding landscape?
   Moorland or valleys; flat or hilly terrain, forests, agricultural or industrial areas, cultural and historical connections

❀ What is the climate?
   Which direction does the area face (e.g. south-facing)?
   How will this direction influence the climate of the garden?
   What is the altitude?
   What kind of rainfall can be expected?
   How do light and shade affect the area?

A concrete surface can be broken up and transformed into living space

A few weeks after the transformation

By the third summer, everything is in full bloom

Is the area particularly susceptible to frost? From which direction does the wind most often blow?

❀ What is the geology of the area?

What are the ratios of soil, sand and stone?

What is the pH value of the soil? (you can have the pesticide content of the soil determined by a specialist)

Are there swampy areas or moorland areas?

Are there natural boulders?

Has building material or rubbish been dumped there?

❀ Who will use the garden — and how?

How old are the people for whom the garden is planned?

What is their social environment?

Where should the entrance, supply routes and emergency paths be placed?

## ⌐ Action guidelines

❀ How can the people who take an area under their protection develop a continuing sense of responsibility and the willingness to protect and care for it?

❀ How can they train their observation skills and who will help them do this?

❀ How can this new area be protected?

❀ Should it be enclosed by a fence, hedges, dry walls or embankments?

❀ How can the diversity of species be maintained or expanded? Think about nesting material for animals, beds for plants, etc.

❀ How can an ecosystem be supported in order to increase the number of species in the new area?

❀ How can a lack of balance in the animal and plant world be recognized and corrected?

❀ Which spots are preferred by plants?

❀ Which paths do animals prefer?

❀ Which areas do children and adults prefer? For example, worn paths, natural places for climbing, balancing, resting, playing in the mud, splashing or building.

## ⌐ Conclusions

In teaching, as in holistic medicine, you have to address people *where they are* and as whole beings. It's the same with outdoor areas: they must be approached as a whole organism. Only then can we understanding what has settled there, and how it would like to live.

In addition, we must consider what kind of atmosphere we want to create, and what we want the future to hold for our children in this area.

All of the following aspects must be considered, and are closely connected:

❀ protection of nature
❀ movement and play areas
❀ resting and private areas
❀ aesthetic design
❀ experience with the elements of nature
❀ areas for fruit, vegetables and herbs
❀ flower and shrub areas

## Landscaping Ideas

Using the park in Wiehl (see next page) and some other projects as examples, here are some landscape ideas that can be done with children and adults working together. At the same time it will become clear how the citizens of Wiehl have adopted this new park as their own.

# Developing the Park in Wiehl

LEGEND

1 Willow arbour

2 Layered tree trunk wall

3 Round wood hill for climbing

4 Clay hill for climbing and building

5 Clay oven

6 Stone building site

7 Wood building site

8 "Benjes hedges"

   a) Double twig-layer wall with trees

   b) Twig-layer wall between supporting stakes

   c) Woven hedge

   d) Loose bushes

9 Climbing tree

10 Nesting wall

11 Trellis hedge

12 Charcoal arbour

13 Arbour building site

14 Water source

15 Tree with benches

16 Round wood spiral for climbing
   and sitting

17 Barbecue site

18 Wooden pavement

19 Natural stone pavement

## — Layered tree trunk wall

In city gardens and nurseries, there are always large numbers of tree trunks. They're usually dumped as waste at great financial expense and can therefore be acquired cheaply, often for nothing. They can be sawed into different lengths and layered with soil into an interesting wall, which provides a new living space for plants, animals and people. It can also serve as an effective sound barrier.

## — Climbing wall

Place different lengths of tree stumps vertically into the ground. You should use hardwood such as fruit trees, beech, ash and oak. The spaces between the stumps should be carefully filled with soil so that the children don't trip or entangle themselves.

## — Tree stump spiral for climbing and sitting

Dig a spiral ditch, about 18" (50cm) deep, and fill it with a base of gravel. Then place hardwood stumps vertically into the ditch and fill up the remaining spaces with soil. The tree stumps can get gradually higher towards the middle of the spiral.

## ⌐ Twig layer wall

Hermann and Heinrich Benjes developed this particular wall using twigs; the walls are generally known in Germany as "Benjes hedges." They create a living space for birds which carry the seeds of many different berries to the area, which creates new life. They tend to develop into a very thick strip of hedge.

*Depending on the area and twig supply available, Benjes hedges can be built from twigs in two rows (above) or in one row (below)*

*Building with many kinds of leftover stones*

## ⌐ Building with stone

You can often find natural stones in disused quarries, and they can be collected and used for playing and building. A dry stone wall can be built from natural stones, which serves not only as a border, but as another living space.

*Tip:* sharp eyes can often find interesting materials in stonemasons' shops.

A SERPENT SEAT
During the family retreat shown in the photographs on the next page, all age groups worked together to create a splendid giant "serpent seat" from frost-resistant stones and leftover tiles. People who were good with their hands willingly agreed to work with children and teenagers who were eager to test both their physical strength and their talents. Other adults joined the group and worked with materials that were new to them.

They dug a ditch 30" (80cm) deep and filled it with a frost protection mixture and a concrete base as the foundation for the serpent. The entire

◄ *Planted fence: If there is only a small space available, a wire fence planted with berry bushes, such as raspberries or blackberries, can divide or edge the area*

*Mixing frost-resistant mortar* ➤

construction site had to be covered with a tent as protection from the constant rain. The body of the serpent was put together with various kinds of stone that had been contributed by different construction companies. Frost-resistant mortar was mixed, and the helpers soon had a good sense of the right consistency for the masonry work. Everyone was quite surprised that they were able to successfully apply the fine surface, cut the tiles to fit, and decorate the serpent with a wonderfully colourful skin. At the end of the retreat week, the project was dedicated in a special ceremony.

*Decorating the final surface* ◀

▼ *Expert mosaic tile cutters*

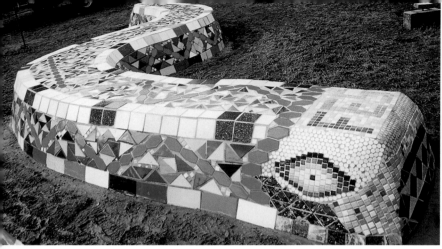

*The project is dedicated in a special ceremony*

## ⌐ Building with wood

The area for building with wood should be near the area for building with stone, because the materials complement each other well. Beams, logs, pieces of board, round wood, squared timber and special branches can be collected.

A layered wood wall made of squared timber (see p. 43) can serve as an edging to the area.

## ⌐ A root mountain

Large chunks of root collected while clearing an area can be placed together to create a "root mountain." In time, this will become a very popular home for small animals and plants.

*Particularly large roots can be positioned as imaginative sculptures in the area. Children like to sit or climb on them, or polish the roots with a strong brush. They love to touch the unusual root growth.* ➤

46

## ⌐ Nesting places for insects and bats

To build a wattle and daub nesting house under eaves or other shelter, braid some willow twigs together and stand them on end. Wrap a layer of wet clay about 4" (10cm) wide around the willow twigs and top the structure with a "mushroom cap" of clay. Then poke holes 1/10" or less (1–10mm) diameter into the clay. The clay will dry out and crumble away in time due to the weather, but the structure can be soaked again and the broken parts of the wall repaired. Bumblebees, hermit bees and hermit wasps like these nesting houses.

Nesting walls can be made with clay or pieces of wood (see photographs 1–3, p. 48). Nesting boxes for birds and bats can also be placed there (see drawing and photograph, p. 49). Climbing plants such as knotgrass, honeysuckle and ivy like to climb on wood; they can be used to protect the entrance of the houses.

The adjacent side-bar contains helpful information about wild bees and wasps as well as building instructions for appropriate nesting aids.

*Nesting places for solitary insects*

## ⌐ Nesting help for wild bees and wasps

Biodiversity is the first prerequisite for a stable ecological balance in a garden, and therefore also the most effective way to protect plants. The least-noticed insects play a decisive role. These numerous small helpers can be supported by creating living spaces such as a hedge, a pile of wood, or a meadow, and especially by planting many kinds of flowering plants. With some species, nesting aids are helpful. This is especially true for one of the largest groups of insects — the hymenoptera — which includes bees and wasps.

### SUPPORTING BEES AND WASPS?

Supporting wasps might seem strange at first to gardeners. But the majority of our bee and wasp species are neither pests nor nuisances. Bees and wasps pollinate the garden, and wasps help to control damaging plant-eating insects.

Most varieties of bees and wasps have no families but are solitary. Because they have no family to defend, they are not aggressive. The females build nesting tunnels in rotted wood, old fence posts, hollow stems of plants, gaps in stone, sand ditches or paths, and care for their brood without the help of other members of the species.

The food supply for the larvae consists either of pollen and nectar or, with most wasps, of stunned insects and caterpillars. After the chambers are filled with food, they are sealed with materials such as clay, resin or leaves.

In the past few years, the population of solitary bees and wasps in the wild has been severely diminished. This has been caused by the use of pesticides and the elimination of their habitat (food and breeding places). Knowing what they need to live, we can effectively help the threatened insects in our gardens with some simple measures.

## NESTING AIDS MADE OF WOOD

Hardwood blocks, tree slices or trunks (oak, beech, acacia or fruitwood) with holes drilled into them, make good nesting places. The holes should have varying diameters between $1/100$–$1/10$" (1–10mm) and depths of 2–4" (5–10cm). The holes should be horizontal.

You can also tie together hollow stems and twigs of elderberry or reeds in a bundle for hanging.

These insect homes should be hung or placed in a sunny spot that is protected from the wind. If the conditions are right, these homes will get used even on a balcony in the city.

## INCLUDING NOURISHING PLANTS AND AVOIDING POISON

Cracks in dry stone walls or open sand surfaces — such as paths in the garden — will be used by some species as nesting spots. It's important to have pollen-rich meadows, flower beds and wild herb patches as sources of nourishment. Refrain completely from using poisonous chemicals such as insecticides and herbicides so as not to endanger the bees and wasps.

*1.–3. A nesting wall of wood. Solitary insects have laid their eggs in glass tubes on the shelf (3); interested observers can take the shelf out of the nesting box (2).*

48

◄ Bat boxes can be constructed from unfinished wood using the measurements indicated. Avoid drafty cracks. Roughen the back wall so that the animals can hold on to the wood. The box should not be sealed or painted, or else the bats will not use it.

A bat box is attached to the wall of a house. Bat boxes should be hung as high as possible and grouped with several other bat boxes.

## ⌐ A willow arbour

This willow project is one that's appropriate for children. You'll find others in other books, but always check that a project is suitable for the age group.

Willow structures need to be placed outdoors where there is good light and moisture. The willow is a wood that needs light, and, given that its natural habitat is near rivers, we can see that it also needs a great deal of water.

There are many kinds of willow. The best kinds for a willow arbour are ones with long, straight shoots with few branches, for example the *Salix lanceolata* (the willow with lancet-like leaves) or *Salix viminalis* (the twisted willow). Bushy willows with many branches are not as useful.

49

*A willow storage area. The willow shoots are closely layered and protected by a woven fence which stops them from freezing. They must also be protected from drying out in the sun or wind.*

*In the foreground, a "beheaded" willow after being cut back*

Willows should ideally be cut back between the beginning of October and the end of February. They should not be cut after the start of March because the pussy willows are the first spring nourishment for bees. Willow branches are also often used by birds to build their nests, so be careful not to disturb them.

If you need to store cut willow branches, for example because the ground is still frozen, layer the branches in a protected area, and cover them with organic material such as leaves, straw, hay or snow.

Willow branches may be available from:
- ❀ public cemeteries and public gardens
- ❀ road maintenance departments
- ❀ water departments
- ❀ forestry departments
- ❀ horticultural agencies

When you're asking for natural materials such as wood, it's a good idea to take along some pictures in order to explain what kind of structure is planned. The people you are asking are unfortunately not always open to landscaping ideas for nature gardens; however, if you explain that it's for a children's garden, they're normally willing to listen and offer help.

PREPARING THE GROUND FOR A WILLOW ARBOUR

*The sitting circle:*

❀ Mark out the desired size with a circle of plants; the bottom should be at least 2.75 yd (2.5m) in diameter if 20 children are to sit there.

❀ Using earth, create a backrest and build up a step for sitting on, about the height of a child's chair.

❀ Cover the ground with wood chips, gravel or natural paving stones to make a dry floor surface.

❀ Use natural paving stones or wooden posts to edge the seat surface.

❀ If needed, use cushions or carpet tiles as protection against the cold.

PREPARING THE PLANTS FOR A WILLOW ARBOUR

On the outside of the round earth embankment, dig holes about 16" (40cm) apart with a stake-hole digger; the holes should be about a quarter as deep as the length of the willow cuttings (in other words, cuttings that are 4 yards (4m) long need holes that are 1 yard (1m) deep). The holes should be considerably wider than the diameter of the willow branches. Sharpen the end of the branches with a knife, or cut on a slant with garden shears and place them into the holes. Fill the remaining empty space with sand. During dry weather, the willow plants can be watered, and the water will seep down through the sand to the deepest roots.

In addition to the thicker main cuttings, a number of smaller willow branches of varying lengths should be placed into holes, bent diagonally across each other, and woven together with the smaller neighbouring branches (see photo on p. 54, bottom left). They can also be bound together with natural material that should disappear naturally after one growing season.

◄ *A round willow conversation pit (4 yard or 4m diameter) immediately after construction. Everyone loves it straightaway.*

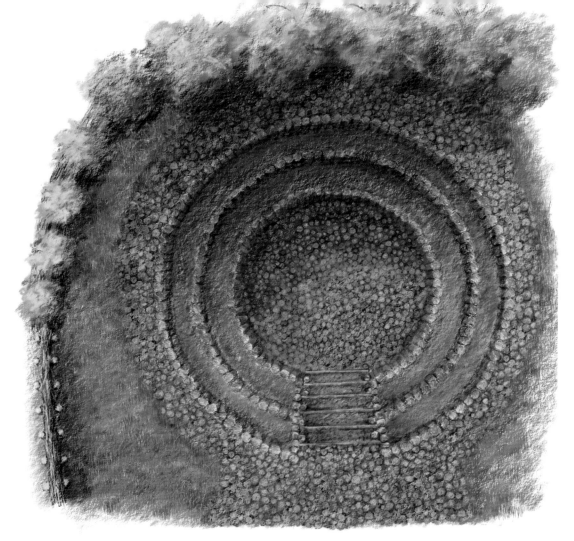

A conversation pit with three steps dug into the ground. The upper level and the inner foot space are covered with wood chips. The lower and middle steps are edged with small wooden posts. The quiet atmosphere is deepened by planting a hedge around the outside.

A sitting wall built up into three steps and edged inside with small wooden posts ➤

# Willow arbour sitting circle

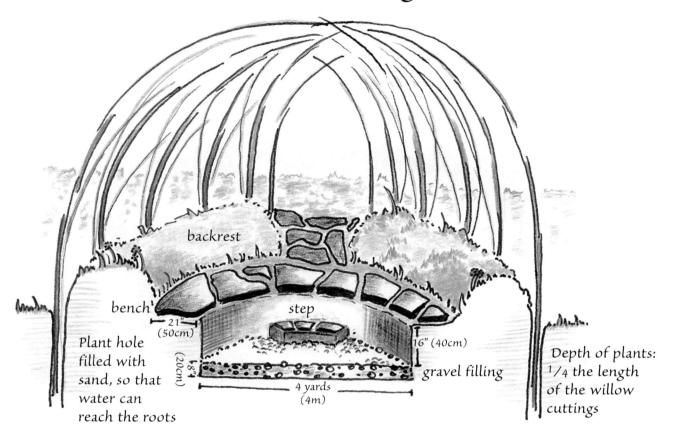

backrest

bench       step

21"
(50cm)

Plant hole
filled with
sand, so that
water can
reach the roots

8"
(20cm)

16" (40cm)

gravel filling

4 yards
(4m)

Depth of plants:
1/4 the length
of the willow
cuttings

Diagonal weaving is much more durable than horizontal weaving which uses cut-off, rootless — and therefore dead — willow branches. In addition, horizontal weaving encourages children to try to climb, which can ruin the entire structure.

All willow structures can be varied with the additional planting of other wild bushes such as hazelnut, elderberry or climbing roses.

The natural structure provides a new attractive living space for birds, insects and small animals — and people — with its colourful, thick, branching blossoms, leaves and fruits, and their associated fragrances.

When the arbour plantings have grown for a few years, the longest shoots can be bound together overhead in the middle. The smaller side shoots can be continually woven together diagonally.

A round willow arbour with earth steps (see photo p. 51) has a very cosy atmosphere. The round shape in a shady place encourages communication; even the most hyperactive child has no problem listening quietly to a story here, because the storyteller's words echo back as if from the earth itself.

▲  *A small round willow seat in the Children's Nature and Garden Centre, built in 1996 . . .*

▲  *. . . after two years an ideal spot for team conferences*

*Diagonal weaving (above) has an advantage over the horizontal weaving (right) in that all of the woven branches touch the ground, form roots, and continue to grow. Branches that do not touch the ground become dry and brittle and eventually rot away.*

Giant willow structures can be formed from bundles of branches. Right, construction of an arbour using this technique. ➤

PHOTOGRAPHS BELOW. The willow branch bundle technique is used to build the Auer World Palace near Bad Sulza in Germany, as part of a large intercultural project

## — *Making a spring flute from a willow branch*

1. You will need a branch as thick as a finger with a straight, smooth central section, about 4" (10cm) long, between two buds. The bud on the thinner end will be cut off cleanly.

2. Cut the mouthpiece on a slant at this end.

3. Cut the air hole precisely on the other edge, below the slant. The knife should be very sharp so that the cut can be made without leaving splinters.

4. Next, cut the bark around the branch, completely encircling it, about 4" (10cm) from the air hole.

5. Wet the whole flute with saliva and carefully tap it with the blunt end of the knife until the bark loosens from the wooden core. This is best done on your knee while kneeling down. Be careful not to split the bark.

6. Now turn the bark carefully, slide it off, and put it to one side.

7. Cut away a flat piece of wood from the notch of the air hole (this will become the air canal).

8. Now, cut off the mouthpiece exactly at the smooth notch.

9. All of the parts, well moistened with saliva, can now be put together onto the wooden core and the spring flute is finished.

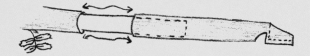

You'll discover that the tone changes when you move the bark. The flute should be placed overnight in water; otherwise it might have dried out by the next day.

One more thing: never cut off too many branches from a tree at once. For environmental reasons, only cut young branches that would be cut off anyway.

*Marianne Frielingsdorf, environment teacher*

## — Play pit

The idea of digging out a hollow in the ground and using the earth to build up a wall around it can be used in many ways. These are cosy retreats where people are protected from noise, wind and unwanted stares. There are no limits to artistic creativity here.

A play pit can be filled with a number of different materials:

❀ sand of different grades, all the way to gravel
❀ round and square pieces of wood
❀ leftover boards and posts
❀ clay
❀ mud
❀ discarded pots, milk jugs, containers, equipment for playing, building, measuring and moving

Native plants, colourful garden shrubs and summer flowers create a wonderful area with lots of insects, and fruit from currant, gooseberry and strawberry bushes just asking to be nibbled.

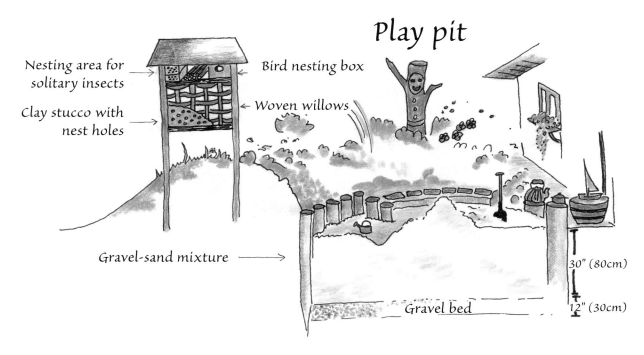

## Play pit

Nesting area for solitary insects

Bird nesting box

Clay stucco with nest holes

← Woven willows

Gravel-sand mixture ⟶

30" (80cm)

12" (30cm)

Gravel bed

# Stone herb garden

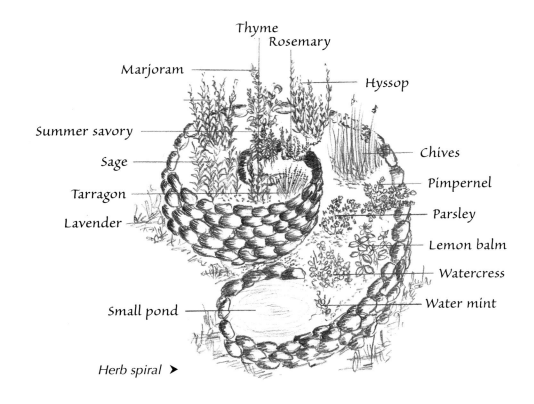

Marjoram
Thyme
Rosemary
Hyssop

Summer savory
Sage
Tarragon
Lavender

Chives
Pimpernel
Parsley
Lemon balm
Watercress
Water mint

Small pond

*Herb spiral* ➤

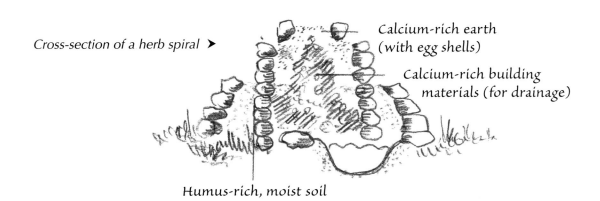

*Cross-section of a herb spiral* ➤

Calcium-rich earth
(with egg shells)

Calcium-rich building
materials (for drainage)

Humus-rich, moist soil

## ⌐ Stone herb garden

A herb spiral makes it possible to grow many herbs well in a very small space. The *Summer* book in this series will include the construction of a spiral stone bed; alternatively, look in other gardening books for details.

▲ *Well-dried egg shells can be ground up and used as a calcium additive for plants that need calcium (lavender, hyssop, summer savory, thyme, marjoram, rosemary and sage).*

*Stone herb beds can also be laid out as a double spiral, as shown here in a Steiner-Waldorf kindergarten. This allows an entire school class to work on the bed at the same time.* ▼

## ⌐ Bed and path edging

Beds and paths can be edged with stones, round or square pieces of wood, or willows. Bed edging should always be raised (see photograph below) so that soil can be built up to a height of 4–8" (10–20cm), whereas path edging should always be set into the ground to prevent stumbling, but at the same time must keep the path material from being washed away by rain.

In both cases, it is important that borders can be clearly seen and touched by children. If there is no clear marking, small children cannot recognize the spot, for instance, where the grass becomes a bed. Clear marking eliminates the need for constant warnings and signs. Small willow fences can also be used as borders — even when they're quite subtle, they do their job (see next page).

Note that all of the structures are made of untreated wood, which should, in time, return to nature in a full cycle. It will feed certain microorganisms — wood moulds, lichen, moss, ferns and other plants. We should continually take stock of our living spaces, to make sure we're using and re-using nature appropriately and creatively.

*This bed is clearly edged with round tree sections* ▼

1

2

3

Willows can be turned into small fences with many variations. They protect flowering plants and make the borders between the bed and the path or grassy area clear to children.

1. Woven fence
2. Arched fence
3. Corner construction with a forked branch

*Woven willow fence: easily made with children if they have already worked with weaving equipment*

Change is especially appealing to children and young people; nothing is more boring than something that never changes. The outdoor area that we have discussed here should continue to change and develop creatively and artistically over a long period of time. The end is not important; the journey's the thing.

## — Paradise garden

We rarely, of course, get the opportunity to take over an entire park. It's better, then, to think about creating a space in a more modest area.

Take an inner-city kindergarten, for example, on the fourth floor of an apartment house, right next to several major roads. The kindergarten does not have an outdoor area at all, except for a small balcony with a roof over it. This is, however, a paradise garden.

A wooden sandbox enclosure measuring 1 yd (1m) square has been divided diagonally. On one side, it's filled with an inviting mix of sand and gravel. Four children can fit in it. On the other side, there is crumbling, fragrant, dark brown potting soil. Flowers can be planted there.

The good potting soil is gathered from the "worm-wandering box" (see description p. 63). This serves not only as a home for earthworms, but also as a seat for the children.

Narrow wooden planter boxes stand around the floor of the balcony producing courgettes (zucchini), tomatoes, cucumber, peppers and onions. Three proud sunflowers are growing in a protected corner, and the nasturtium with its glowing yellow, orange and red flowers climbs vigorously over the balcony railing.

In one of the planter boxes, a scarlet runner bean plant is climbing up the drain pipe to the floor above; the neighbours are delighted. Fragrant herbs are growing in flower boxes hanging outside the railing: lavender, marjoram, thyme, lemon thyme, sage, summer savory and hyssop. They have a marvellous variety of flowers and provide food for many insects.

In the semi-shade of the inner balcony railing, near the rain barrel, flowerpots are waiting with chives and parsley for sandwiches, and peppermint and lemon balm for tea.

In another wooden barrel water, water horsetails, marsh plants and sword lilies are growing.

On the sunny side of the balcony there are a number of nesting places, protected from the rain, for solitary insects; they're made of clay or round and square pieces of wood (see p. 47). There is even a bumblebee box, handmade out of wood and concrete for a social species of bumblebee, which stands waiting for inhabitants. A potato box or strawberry pot (see p. 64) would also be ideal here.

This kind of airy garden paradise is, of course, totally dependent on the loving care of big and little gardeners alike. Everything can only grow and develop if the differing water needs of the individual plants are constantly checked by looking and feeling. Adults must show children how to do this, and it is excellent training for their senses. You can't just say to children, "go water the flowers." Experiments in trial and error can lead to dead plants. Gardening becomes an art under difficult — almost artificial — conditions with the highest demands on the continuity of care. A child can only learn this art by imitating adults.

A butterfly breeding box would be the crown jewel of a balcony like this one (see *Summer* in this series of books).

This flower pot nest for a bumblebee family can also be placed in a planter box on the balcony. The flower pot lies on its side with a small entrance pipe in the bottom; the top opening is covered with a wooden board. The whole structure is protected with a large piece of bark.

Nesting places for solitary insects. They can easily be installed in a sunny corner of the balcony.

## ~ Earthworms — compost in a worm box

French peasants had a saying, "God knows how fertile soil is made, and He entrusted His secret to the earthworms."

Earthworms create fertile soil because they improve the structure of the earth. They live in close symbiosis with an army of other micro-organisms, bacteria and moulds. These organisms, in the digestive tract of the earthworms, are essential for the production of earthworm humus.

### THE EARTHWORMS' CONTRIBUTION
*With the help of earthworms:*
* the earth is aerated;
* the earth holds more water;
* roots can grow more deeply into the earth to take up essential minerals and water;
* the structure of the earth is improved;
* nourishment is made available to plants;
* organic and clay particles are mixed.

A clay-humus mixture comes from organic matter and the products of decay. The nourishing substances are not washed away even by strong rains. With the help of micro-organisms, earthworms turn garden waste into plant food. Worm excrement contains seven times more phosphate, eleven times more potassium, and five times more nitrogen than the surrounding earth.

*Earthworms can be encouraged in these ways:*
* Avoid using chemical pesticides. Use mineral fertilizer only as needed as an addition to organic fertilizer.

* Loosen and aerate the earth with a pitchfork rather than with a spade to protect living things, including earthworms. The layers of earth remain intact.

* Composting, mulching and fertilizing the entire area with organic matter provides earthworms and all of the other organisms in the earth with adequate nourishment, and keeps the earth loose and uniformly moist.

### Earthworms eliminate waste
The "manure worm," known by worm growers as the "Tennessee Wiggler" or the "Red Californian," is best suited to composting garden and kitchen waste. All organic kitchen waste, including the coffee filter and all garden and fruit waste, can be composted.

### COMPOSTING IN A WORM-WANDERING BOX
An earthworm box is an alternative to a compost box. A small one can fit into a courtyard or a very small garden. An earthworm box does not smell, needs very little space, and will not attract mice or rats.

A box with three chambers is a good size for an average family. If space is a problem, you can use a box with two chambers. The location should be shady or partially shady.

Dig a hole 25–30" (60–70cm) deep. Smooth and level the ground at the bottom of the hole. Cover the bottom tightly with cinder blocks (concrete blocks containing vertical holes). This prevents condensation and keeps out burrowing animals. The compost material will be in contact with the ground, and, in case of frost, the earthworms can take refuge by going through the vertical holes into deeper earth. The upper edges of the blocks must be exactly level, so that there are no spaces between them and the wooden framework above.

Next construct a wooden box to fit the hole and place it into the ground. Inside the box, build the dividing wall (in the case of three chambers, the two dividing walls) from cinder blocks with holes oriented horizontally so that the earthworms can wander from one chamber to another. The dividing walls can be mortared with concrete.

Because compost worms only come to the upper layers when it is dark, the box should be covered. The cover also protects the compost from drying out, and from rain, and prevents rats and mice from getting in.

### Composting in the Box

Place a layer of organic material, about 4" (10cm) thick, into one chamber and cover with rock dust. Add compost worms and continually feed with more organic material. Onion skins and coffee grounds, in particular, are delicacies for worms. Every once in a while, the individual layers should be covered with rock dust. If a great deal of leaves or straw and wooden waste is placed into the worm box, some bone meal should be added. Diseased plant cuttings or fruit should not be composted.

When one chamber is full, start filling the second chamber. When the first chamber has been turned into humus by bacteria, earthworms and other organisms will be attracted by the smell of the organic materials from the second chamber and will wander through the holes in the bricks to this chamber. Depending on the size of the chamber, the finished product, the "worm compost," can be harvested after six to ten months. This compost is especially rich and should be distributed only in a thin layer onto garden soil, flower beds or flower boxes.

*The potato plants must be covered with earth again and again*

## — Potato box

Line a wooden vegetable box (see photograph above) with a heavy sheet of plastic and cover with a 4" (10cm) layer of good earth. Place a ready-to-sprout potato in each corner of the box and cover with earth. Water, but do not overwater. When little leaves push up through the earth, cover the small plants with earth again, just as is done in the fields.

In September, the many tiny little potatoes are ready to be harvested, and are so tasty as to be worth their weight in gold. A delicious thanksgiving soup can be made from the potatoes along with ripe beans, kohlrabi, cabbage, carrots and herbs.

*Clay pots with pocket-like side openings can also be planted with fragrant herbs*

## ⌐ Strawberry pots

In a clay strawberry pot, the strawberry plants push out through the side openings towards the light. They grow simple white flowers, which eventually turn into aromatic fruit. The fruit is often so popular, it hardly has time to ripen.

## ⌐ Keeping pets

If you're lucky enough to have a large natural out-door area, you could consider keeping small pets. On page 66 is a drawing of a small animal stable on wheels — as a child has imagined it — for a few chickens, guinea pigs, rabbits or hamsters.

In schools and other institutions for children, small pets are best kept "on loan" for a few weeks or months; the best time for this is the period between holidays during the summer months. Planning should involve thinking in advance about how to care for the animals over the weekend, and how they can be returned to their owners.

For a large school or kindergarten, keeping honeybees is recommended but you must have an expert who can care for them, and a quiet spot with a nourishing environment. You should ask your local beekeeping association for advice on this kind of project. There's more about this in the chapter on beekeeping (see p. 82).

*Farms can act as natural counterbalances to children's isolation from the environment. Some biodynamic farms welcome groups of children if there is time in between their work.*

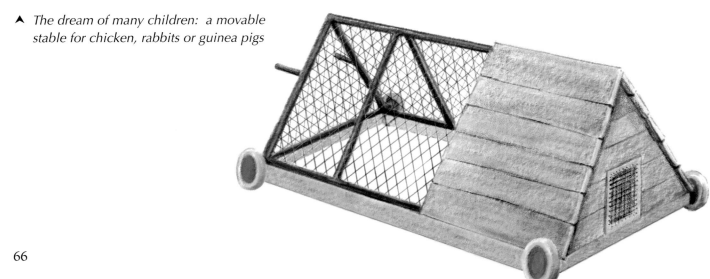

▲ *The dream of many children: a movable stable for chicken, rabbits or guinea pigs*

Biodynamic farms are a rock in times of ecological change. Some farms, such as Birkenhof in Germany, are committed to being self-sustaining. This means that in winter, their animals are kept in open barns where they can move around rather than being tethered in stalls. The feed for the animals is provided by the farm's own grounds and fields, which are fertilized with the well-composted manure of the farm's own animals. All of the farm's products are sold in the farm shop.

*Birch branches are cut, bundled and dried during the summer. In the winter, they are ground and mixed with hay for their nourishing properties.*

◄ *A portable small animal stable with a fresh air section and a covered sleeping section. It goes without saying that animals living in this kind of stable are totally dependent upon the consistent loving care of humans.*

A well-landscaped living space, in harmony with nature, can free up children's creative imaginations and life forces in a truly remarkable way. We simply need to give them enough time and space for their individual development, and offer experienced guidance when necessary. When children create a living space for plants and animals, they are taking important steps on their journey from being a limited individual to a citizen of the world.

## April does what she wants

Once upon a time there was a Little Wind who owned nothing but a large, empty sack. He went to Summer, who was getting ready for the trip to Earth along with her servants, June, July and August.

He said, "Dear Summer, please take me with you! I want to blow a little just once."

"I'm so sorry," said Summer, "this summer I don't need any more wind. But perhaps you can come along next year."

But because Little Wind looked so sad, Summer gave him a little bit of sunshine so that he could warm up. Little Wind put the sunshine into his sack and went to Autumn, who was mixing wonderful colours for the trees with the help of September, October and November.

"Dear Autumn," said Little Wind, "please take me with you! I want to blow just once."

"Hmmmm," answered Autumn. "You're very small, dear Wind, and I need strong winds."

But because he was sorry for Little Wind, he gave him a little bit of rain. Little Wind put it all into his sack and went to Winter.

"Dear Winter," he said, "please take me with you, when you go to Earth! I want to blow a lot just once."

"Well," said Winter to his servants, "let's see what he can do!" December, January and February told Little Wind to blow the snow from the mountains. But as much as he blew, there was too much snow. He couldn't do it.

"I can see," said Winter, "that you're too weak for us and can't take the cold. But I'll give you a little bit of snow, so you can practice, and next year I'll take you with me."

Little Wind put the snow into his sack and went to Spring.

"Dear Spring," he asked, "can you use me? I'm sure I can blow very nicely."

"What do you think, my friends," said Spring to March, April and May, "does anyone need a little wind?"

April came up, smiled brightly, and she said, "Yes indeed, I've been looking for a nice small wind for a long time."

Little Wind was thrilled! He hugged April and blew a soft "thank you" into her ear. That tickled April so that she had to laugh and sneeze at the same time. But she liked Little Wind, and, when the time came, they went to Earth together.

"Okay, Little Wind," said April, "I have a lot of work to do with the flowers and trees. But you can blow over the meadow and paths and melt the last snow."

April went about her job and Little Wind did what he had been told. He blew softly and warmly so that the snow melted and flowed in small brooks through the meadow.

But the children came running and called out, "Oh, our lovely snowman; he's all melted!"

"I can fix that," said Little Wind. He took a little bit of snow out of his sack and blew it across the land. This made the children very happy.

But the farmer in the field was angry. "Oh, you bad snow, you're destroying my seeds!" And little Gretl was crying, "Oh, my beautiful flowers; they'll all freeze!"

"I can fix that," said Little Wind. He took a little bit of sunshine out of his sack and blew it

across the land. This made the farmer and Gretl very happy.

But the people in the town said, "Oh, this heat! If it's this warm in April, what will it be like in the summer?"

"I can fix that," said Little Wind. He took a little bit of rain out of his sack and let it fall onto the Earth.

But now the people started to complain. "What awful weather!" they cried. "You can't even step out of your house without getting your feet wet!"

Now the Little Wind was angry. He blew as hard as he could, blew windows open and closed, and blew people's hats off their heads. And in between he reached into his sack and blew across the Earth whatever he grabbed: rain, snow, and sunshine.

When April discovered this, she stamped in rage, grabbed Little Wind, and shouted, "Oh, you useless thing, you windbag! Did I tell you to annoy the whole world?"

Little Wind began to cry and finally told April why he had done all this. April had to laugh. She shook her head and said, "These people — you just can't do anything right in their eyes. But don't worry, my little friend, just help me some more!"

Since that time, April takes the Little Wind with her to Earth. Little Wind often plays his tricks with us, blows rain and snow into our faces, hits us with his sunshine, and blows away our caps.

April does what she wants with us!

# May

Plant-based
dyes and paints

Milk processing

Beekeeping

# Plant-based dyes and paints

Plant growth in May begins under the zodiac sign of Taurus, the bull (♉). Stems and leaves, in particular, reach full size at this point, and the explosion of growth slows down. Flowers start to form under the sign of Gemini, the twins (♊). Bright, fresh colours appear alongside tender buds.

We can bring some of this array of colour into the kindergarten by making sure that our toys, costumes, cushion covers, sandbags and cloth bags are plant-dyed, to radiate fresh spring colours.

Today we take it for granted that we can buy coloured cloth everywhere. But we also know that the cloth is dyed in large factories using complicated chemical processes. Thus the process of dyeing that people performed for thousands of years using materials from their natural surroundings, without knowledge of modern chemistry, has almost been lost.

Substances for use in dyeing can be found in leaves, flowers, fruit, seeds, bark and plant roots. Cloth made of natural fibres, such as cotton, silk and sheep's wool in unspun, spun, twisted and woven form, can be dyed naturally with plant extracts to give it a vibrant new colour.

Note that not every kind of material absorbs dye well. New cloth should be washed in very hot water and rinsed well to remove the starch. We will not cover natural dyes made from animal or mineral materials here.

In order to produce dyes that are resistant to bleeding in water or fading in sunlight, the cloth

*Cotton cloth dyed yellow with birch leaves*

must be treated before it is dyed. Depending on the thickness of the cloth, a 1–2 percent alum solution is used to help fix the dye (100–200g of alum from the chemist to 2.5 gal (10l) of water).

Mix the alum with hot water in a bucket, stirring with a wooden spoon. Place the cloth loosely in the bucket for 30 minutes. For a deeper colour, the cloth can be boiled with the fixing solution. Rinse the cloth, wring it out, and dip it into the simmering dye mixture. The fixing solution opens the textile fibres so that they can absorb the dye.

## Making Dyes

In order to release the dye substances in the plants, chop up the chosen plant parts, soak them overnight, and boil for two hours the next day. The dye solution is then ready. If the cloth is stirred carefully in the solution, the dye will be absorbed uniformly. When the desired shade of colour is achieved, remove the cloth from the solution, wring it out, dry and iron it.

Children normally show great interest and enthusiasm for dyeing pieces of cloth in plant solutions from the field, forest, meadow and garden. Through this, they subconsciously develop a relationship with the plant world. Early experiences like this can be developed later on and related to school subjects in a more intellectual way.

There are many natural dye substances, because everything organic contains dye characteristics. In the following overview, note that a particular flower, leaf or root does not always produce the exact colour you expect. The precise colour and intensity can vary greatly depending on the plant location, weather and the time of harvesting. When working with small children, it is important to use plants that can be found in their immediate surroundings.

## Colour Chart for Plant-Dyeing

* *Yellow:* goldenrod, tansy, camomile, sunflower, broom, hazelnut leaves, onion skins
* *Yellow-green:* birch leaves, eagle fern, meadow chervil, carrot leaves, tomato leaves, elderberry leaves, ash, apple tree bark (from felled trees)
* *Reddish yellow:* greater celandine, broad-leafed ampher (ox tongue)
* *Dark brown:* walnut hull
* *Brown:* dandelion roots, horse chestnut leaves, oak bark
* *Pink:* willow bark, pear tree bark (from felled trees)
* *Light red:* bedstraw, woodruff
* *Blue:* dyer's woad
  Extracting blue dye from plants is difficult and you shouldn't try it without experience. Dyes taken from dark berries or from red cabbage will fade when exposed to light.
* *Poppy ink:* Poppy flowers usually wilt very fast in summer. The fallen blossoms can be collected around noon for four or five days. Fill a small bowl with the flowers and pour a small amount of boiling water over them. For a large double handful of poppy flowers, you'll need an egg-cup of boiling water. Knead the flowers in the water and strain them a day later. The light-pink ink darkens to dark pink if an iron pen nib is used.

*Marianne Frielingsdorf, environment teacher*

73

# Characteristics of Plants Used for Dyeing

* Plants that grow in *dry stony soil* have more dye content than those that grow in moist, cool soil.

* Plants that grow during *warm summers* have more colour intensity than those that grow during cool and wet summers.

* The dyes in *slow-growing plants* are more long-lasting than those in fast growing plants.

* *Leaves* contain a larger amount of dye substance shortly *before budding.*

* The colour content in *stems* is often strongest shortly *after blossoming.*

* *Buds* contain the most dye substance directly *before opening* or soon *afterwards.*

* *Tree bark* (please take only from recently felled trees) contains the most dye substance when the tree is *in full sap,* when the buds open in the spring. The *inner bark,* the bast, has the deepest colour. The bark of *young trees* contains more dye content than that of older trees and the bark of the *thin branches* more than that of the trunk.

* *Plant roots* have the most dye content when they have *finished growing* in the autumn.

* Most plants produce more dye if they are *dried* rather than fresh.

*Note:* Not everything can be harvested in May, so it's a good idea to keep a supply of specific dye plants on hand. If dye plants cannot be harvested in person, they can be purchased from specialty suppliers.

Experimenting with these very simple dyeing methods will produce amazing results, and the children will be delighted. Have fun with colour activities! Note that textiles dyed with plant dyes are only partially resistant to fading. They should be dyed again every year in May.

If children go to kindergarten for three years, they will experience the same activity, at a certain time of the year, three times in all, and can absorb it. The first year they will watch; the second year they will participate; and the third year they will be able to do the dyeing largely on their own. Rhythm and repetition are important educational elements.

## Painting with Plant-Based Paints

Dye from plants can be used for painting; however, it's better to use industrially produced plant-based paints for painting with watercolours in kindergartens and schools. Children like to prepare them anew each time and to mix them with natural resin emulsion.

In a time when chemically produced paints are aggressive, loud and sometimes extremely damaging to the environment, plant-based paints are quieting and comfortably invigorating for the eye. The human sense of sight, especially in children, is often exhausted by back-lit advertising, neon lighting and too much television. Being surrounded by, and painting with, plant-based paints allows the eyes to develop a very fine sense of differentiation.

# The Invigorating Effect of Plant Colours

Every year, when nature reawakens, colour comes back into our lives. Soon after the first light of day, green grass and many colourful buds arise; it is one of the wonders of our world — and not only for children. After winter's break from colour, the brown earth turns toward the sun, and when the green plant world can grow no further towards the sky, the beauty of leaf shapes gives way to the splendid colour of flowers and their fragrance.

Flower colours — ranging from delicate to strong, but always invigorating — move us deeply and fill us with joy, because we sense a personal connection. In our souls, we too have ever-new colours caused by our actions, and these colours surround us. In this sense, we're right to speak of someone as "glowing" or "pale," or to say that someone "sees red."

In contrast to the actively living colours in us and in nature are the synthetically-coloured surroundings in which many of our children live. The natural colour break of winter, during which the eye can rest and we can personally regroup, no longer exists. Screaming, solid colours demand our attention. They push us into action but allow for nothing new. It is as if indigestible stones are given to us instead of bread, because there's nothing alive in these colours which result from synthetic, lifeless processes.

We no longer notice what is special in our everyday routines. Our eyes constantly demand new attractions and new colours, which, however, do not stimulate our interest. On the contrary, our interest becomes restless and our feeling for beauty eventually shrinks.

In this way, we no longer see the colour of the shadows, or the unbelievably rich nuances of green during a walk. Instead, the colours of particular products are fixed in our minds, even in the minds of children. Global products mean it's the same all over the world. Every year, new fashion colours replace old ones, and new patterns replace last year's, otherwise we would become bored with the clothes.

Using plant colours can help to counteract some of these damaging effects. Outer uneasiness and the busy demands of our modern world can be somewhat stilled by surrounding ourselves with natural colours which we've seen made, or of which we know the source. Using plant colours in painting can encourage sensitivity and an inner quietness in a child. Let us give this to our children.

*Alexander Bräutigam, art and speech teacher*

# Milk processing

The greatest profusion of flowers comes towards the end of May under the influence of Gemini, the twins (♊). As the symbol indicates, this is the time that the two genders develop in nature. In plants, this is shown in the development of the male stamen and the female pistil and ovary. The colourful flowers attract bees to collect honey and pollen, in exchange for fertilization.

On a walk to a blooming, fragrant May meadow, you'll see two very different kinds of animals: the bee and the cow.

Honeybees buzz tirelessly from flower to flower, without noticing whether another bee has already sucked up the available nectar. Imagine being a bee: diving into a fragrant sea of colour all day and soaking up pollen and nectar which are many times heavier than your own bodyweight, all to support your bee family.

And what about the cow, feeding and ruminating all day, nourishing itself from the rich meadow and producing large amounts of milk?

Every day our children consume milk products in various forms, and we cannot imagine our daily menu without them. More and more children, however, no longer know where the milk comes from and how it is turned into soft cheese, yoghurt, butter, cheese and cream. For this reason it would be good to visit a cow with a newborn calf, if possible on a farm that keeps its cows properly. There you can explain to the children that the milk only flows if the cow has given birth to a calf.

Grandparents of kindergarten children have collected the following milk recipes. Pasteurized milk from a biodynamic farm should be used, which has been heated to F 161–167° (72–75°C) for 15 to 30 seconds in order to kill bacteria. If you're making curdled milk, yoghurt or kefir, the appropriate cultures must be added; these can be obtained (with instructions) from farmers, cheesemakers, specialized dairies and health food stores.

◄ *After the calf is born, the cow's udder is ready to produce milk*

## The Cow — Serving Humankind Since Ancient Times

The month of May is the most wonderful time in agriculture. The seeds of grain and vegetables have germinated and are growing well, along with wild herbs. There is some peace and quiet before the harvests begin.

Depending on the region and the kind of farm, cows and their calves have been out in the fields for some time. The lambs are getting bigger and are beginning to feed on grass. The bees, too, have their pick of flowers and bring in the first honey harvest.

This is a time of fullness, when everything is bubbling over with life. It's a wonderful time too for everyone who is able to buy direct from a farm. Children in particular enjoy seeing all this, especially the young animals.

In a time when milk and milk products are sold in large quantities, it is difficult to imagine the dark side of all of this richness. Milk and meat, honey and eggs — we're pleased that they are always available. But how is that possible? By breeding and selection on the one hand — but also by certain methods of feeding and maintenance to produce the highest return at the lowest cost. Economic factors determine breeding practices, while at the same time these high performance animals have a low life expectancy. This has resulted in a general susceptibility to disease with some of the following consequences:

❀ Loss of fertility in the female animals
❀ Development problems in the calves
❀ Difficult births for beef cattle
❀ Damage to legs and hooves
❀ Epidemics and mite infections in pigs and bees
❀ Increasing genetic problems in cattle

This decline in health is due in part to the extreme specialization of these animals that happened in the second half of the twentieth century, and and because they have been removed from their natural habitat. There are many one-sided breeding practices which have also contributed: forced increase in milk production; changes to individual body parts such as a flatter pelvis or additional ribs; repeated breeding of mutations (such as double loins) in white-blue Belgian cattle; the introduction of animal species from other regions; and raising only one variety of animal in a particular area.

At this point we should discuss pets. The concept of a pet can include a large variety of animals — from a canary, to a dog and a horse, to a cow — but these animals are all very different. There is a difference between pets and "domestic animals," that is, working animals. A sheepdog, for example, is a domestic animal (rather than a pet) in that it's a working animal — but even then there's a huge difference between it and a cow.

Dogs and cats are the animals most often kept as pets. They are very close to human beings and they lie, literally, at our feet. Howeer they're never very far away from being a wild animal. Except for certain specially bred varieties, dogs and cats can survive without human protection. As much as we tie them to us, they are basically independent of humans.

Cows, on the other hand, are almost completely dependent on humans, even though they're a domestic (working) animal. If we were to send a herd of dairy cows into the woods, they would probably not survive.

On biodynamic farms, there are particular emphases on adequate movement for cattle, and on varied feed (mainly feed that comes directly from the farm). It's important to choose a stable, local breed of animal which is well-adapted to the area.

Breeding should aim to balance production and health, which also leads to longer life. While the average life of a German cow is approximately 4.5 years, cows on environmentally-friendly farms live for an average of 8 years. There are animals on our farm that are 15 years or older and which have produced seven calves.

To ensure the health of domestic animals, we need an approach which doesn't put economics first. It's more important to consider the nature of the animal and to realize that it is always ready to serve people. Gratefulness should come not only from the farmer, but also from the consumer of the milk and honey products.

*Pauline van Royen-Schmidt*
*Eschenhof Farm*

# Milk — Lifeblood of the Child

Milk is the most nourishing drink that there is — whether it be the milk of cows, sheep or goats. Because this drink contains all the nutrients that a human being needs, small children and ill people can be fed for a long time on milk alone.

Raw milk often contains bacteria, which can cause disease; for this reason, small children should never drink unpasteurized milk.

## What can be made from milk?

❀ Boiled, warm milk with honey

❀ Boiled and then cooled milk

❀ *Mixed drinks:* with fruit or fruit juice, especially delicious with grated apples

❀ Cocoa

- *Curdled milk:* pour the milk into bowls or mugs. The flatter the container, the faster the milk will curdle — one to two days, depending on the temperature, until it becomes firm. Delicious with sugar and cinnamon.

- *Soft cheese (quark):* heat curdled milk until the whey has separated from the solids. Place a thin cloth into a sieve and pour the curdled milk through the sieve. The soft cheese is left in the strainer.

- *Whey* is good for many illnesses; you can drink it, or gargle with it, or make a poultice out of it, for example, for blood poisoning and insect bites.

- *Curd cheese:* delicious with milk and any kind of fruit, with a bit of sweetness added. Good for cheesecake, dumplings and soup. Good salty, on bread or with potatoes and casseroles. Mix with milk and salt, add onions, herbs, or tomatoes to taste.

- *Cheeses:* soft and hard cheeses.

- *Cream soup:* cream soups and puddings with oatmeal flakes, rice or semolina

- *Butter:* a stoneware container (see photos opposite) or a large canning jar can substitute for a churn; you just need a wooden board with holes in it that is attached to a handle at least two hands longer than the container. Use another board as the cover, with a hole for the handle. Now butter can be churned. The cream should be at about F 60° (15°C). You can also use an eggbeater or shake the cream in a jar long enough so that the fat and buttermilk separate.

- *Buttermilk* can be enjoyed cold, or in soups or puddings; it can also be poured over hot potatoes and served with many dishes.

  Place the lump of butter into a clean bowl (wooden is best); run water over it; then knead it with a wooden spoon until no more buttermilk appears. Salt can be added if necessary. Put the butter in a butter dish, or make it into decorations. Butter from sweet cream tastes best in May when the cows go back to the fields ("May butter"). Butter from sour cream has a stronger taste, but the cream should not be too old. Of course you can also make butter from bought cream, but then the cream has to be beaten for a longer time.

- *Yoghurt and kefir:* made with cultures added to warm milk.

- *Ice cream:* Take 3½ cups (½ litre) milk, ½ vanilla stick (or 1 teaspoon vanilla extract), 1 teaspoon cornstarch, 2–3 egg yolks, and ½ cup (100g) sugar. Boil the milk, add the starch which has been stirred into a bit of cool milk, and boil both for one minute. Beat the egg yolks and sugar together, and add the hot milk while continuing to beat. Let mixture stand for one minute (do not boil further); pour into containers and freeze.

- *Boiled cheese:* add a pinch of baking soda to one pound of quark (soft cheese); add 1 teaspoon caraway seeds to taste. Knead the quark, cover with a cloth, and let it stand at room temperature until it becomes viscous

and there is no white to be seen (about one week). In a saucepan, brown 1 tablespoon of butter or bacon fat, add the quark mixture, and let it all melt at low heat; then boil briefly and allow to cool.

All of this, and much more, can be made from milk.

*Ruth Hecht, home economics consultant*

▲ *A miniature churn like this can sometimes be found at flea markets. It works quickly and easily.*

*Churning butter requires patience and strength. Any tall, thick-walled stoneware or glass vessel can, with the help of a wooden churner, be transformed into a butter churn. The churner can easily be made by a clever woodworker.*

# Beekeeping

Under certain conditions — in particular, with expert help and positioned in outdoor areas — bees can be observed and cared for in a children's garden. Just as milk is rich in nutrients at this time of year, bees also form precious, flavourful honey in their beehives.

To date, we have had very positive experiences with honeybees in the Children's Nature and Garden Centre, despite continually changing groups of children and adults. During the entire summer last year not one of the approximately 2,000 visitors was stung, even though five bee colonies live in our small outdoor area of 1,100 square metres.

As adults learn more about beekeeping, they can show children how bees live peacefully with each other, and how they work for the good of the community.

Unfortunately, bees now need people for their survival. Attempts to maximize profits have led to the spread of the *varroa* mite from India, which causes a dangerous bee disease. If left untreated it leads to death for bee colonies. If the natural circle of pollination, fruit production, and nourishment is to be continued into the future, humans are needed to help honeybees survive.

## From Forest Bees to Beekeeping

Originally the bee was a forest creature and nested in holes in trees. Human beings soon discovered the sweet honey and began to hunt for bees.

Beekeeping in ancient times amounted to little more than uncontrolled theft of honey and wax. Under dangerous conditions, honeycombs were torn out of cliff walls and caves and the natural bee homes destroyed. Through this exploitation, humans endangered the future of the bee colonies.

It came to an end when people realized that organized beehives increased the possibility of a bee settlement, and a harvest of honey and wax.

In the Middle Ages, forest beekeepers were respected people. Besides protecting the wild forests, they looked for suitable tree trunks and prepared them to be attractive to a swarm of bees, in the hope that they might nest there. They also carried a crossbow, to protect them from honey-loving bears.

Wild beekeeping reached its peak in the fifteenth and sixteenth centuries, when domestic beekeeping and breeding began to take over. It was easier to cut down the hollow tree trunks that had previously housed the bees and bring these "stump beehives" closer to home.

At that time, agriculture was intended only to feed one's own family and so beekeeping was on a small scale. The economic significance of beekeep-

◄ *Frames of wax are used to help bees construct honeycomb in the beehive*

ing grew as science and technology developed, and as scientific interest in bees increased. Knowledge about nest hierarchy, honey storage and, most importantly, renewing the hives led to more effective beekeeping and breeding. Today, these are still the foundation of modern beekeeping.

In the nineteenth century, many teachers and ministers looking for a supplement to their low pay diversified into beekeeping. This reduced the opportunities for professional beekeepers but the teachers' and ministers' research, however, meant that profits in bee products continued to increase.

# The Bee Colony — Structure and Organization

The honeybee is the only one out of 500 kinds of bees in Germany that builds a whole community in which to survive the winter. The community is highly organization with designated tasks. A colony consists of the queen bee, tens of thousands of female worker bees, and, during the summer, several hundred drones. The colony, therefore, consists of many individuals, but they can only survive as members of a single social community. Every colony is a perfectly organized society with genetically fixed behaviour appropriate for the environment, which must include enough food within flying range, and somewhere to nest.

## ⌐ The queen bee

The queen was originally also called the *leader,* because it was thought that she had a leader-function during swarming. She is the source of all offspring of the colony. In her ovaries, the male spermatozoa remain fertile throughout her life. A queen that has mated only leaves the hive to swarm. She is surrounded by her court, the female workers, who feed her with royal jelly, the queen's food. The queen can live for as long as five years but is usually replaced by the colony after two years. Her egg production is greatest during her early years, when she lays up to 2,000 eggs daily. Whether or not a queen will mature from a fertilized egg depends entirely on the feeding of the larva with royal jelly. A queen's larva is in an especially large cell, the "queen's cell," and emerges after sixteen days.

## ⌐ Female workers

A female worker bee develops in 21 days, from a fertilized egg cell to a larva and then the cocoon stage. She is prevented from laying eggs herself by a substance produced by the queen, and she cares for the brood. She only lives for six weeks — only bees born in late fall live longer — and takes on various tasks that arise from the division of labour in the hive community. The bees assigned to producing honey are responsible for about 15 to 20 kilograms per colony. 100 grams of honey requires about one million visits to flowers. In order to produce 500 grams of honey, the worker bees fly about 75,000 miles (120,000km), or three times around the earth.

## ⌐ Drones

The male bees exist solely to fertilize the queen. The mating flight takes place in May. The queen mates with several drones, who have then fulfilled their function and die. The development of a drone takes 24 days. Male bees have no stingers

# The lifecyle of the honeybee

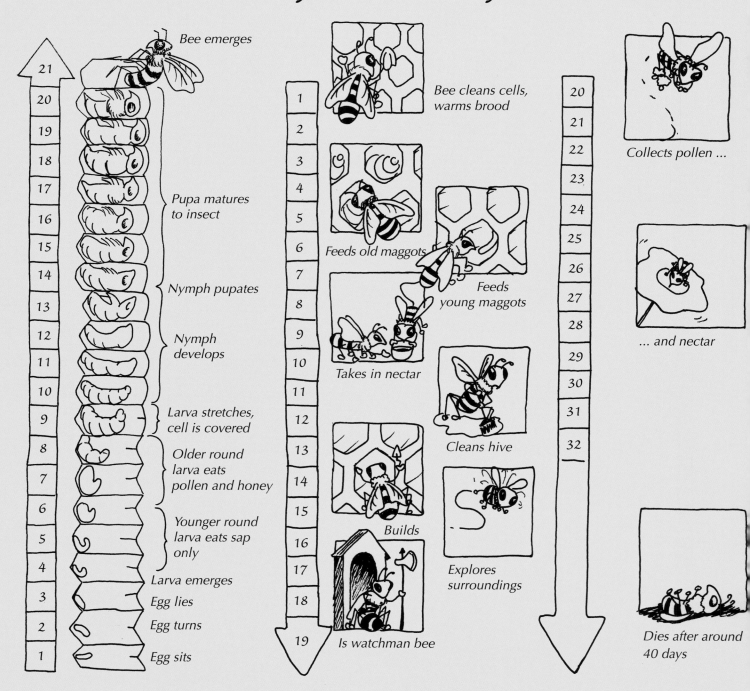

**Development to mature insect**

- 21
- 20
- 19 — Bee emerges
- 18 ⎫
- 17 ⎬ Pupa matures to insect
- 16 ⎭
- 15
- 14 — Nymph pupates
- 13
- 12 — Nymph develops
- 11
- 10
- 9 — Larva stretches, cell is covered
- 8 — Older round larva eats pollen and honey
- 7
- 6 — Younger round larva eats sap only
- 5
- 4 — Larva emerges
- 3 — Egg lies
- 2 — Egg turns
- 1 — Egg sits

**Becomes beehive bee**

- 1 — Bee cleans cells, warms brood
- 2
- 3
- 4
- 5
- 6 — Feeds old maggots
- 7 — Feeds young maggots
- 8
- 9
- 10 — Takes in nectar
- 11
- 12
- 13 — Cleans hive
- 14
- 15 — Builds
- 16
- 17 — Explores surroundings
- 18
- 19 — Is watchman bee

**Becomes collecting bee**

- 20
- 21
- 22 — Collects pollen ...
- 23
- 24
- 25
- 26 — ... and nectar
- 27
- 28
- 29
- 30
- 31
- 32 — Dies after around 40 days

and cannot live without being fed by the worker bees, because they have no organs to collect nectar and honeydew.

## Biology of the Bee

Bees performs an important task for all of nature by pollinating cultivated and wild plants. About 80 percent of our native plants depend upon pollination by insects. A visit by bees during the flowering period leads, in the example of apples and pears for instance, to a better crop and a better balance of sugar and acid.

The honeybee has various tools without which it could not perform its many tasks:

❀ The mouth tools are finely chiselled and can form a tube through which the hairy tongue sucks nectar and honeydew from the flowers.
❀ The strong jaws of the bee function like pliers to cut open pollen bags and knead wax platelets before moulding them into honeycomb.
❀ The forelegs have a kind of spiny comb with which the bee can clean its antennae.
❀ The rear legs have thick hairs on the inside, which form the pollen comb. The pollen basket, into which the pollen is collected, is on the outside of the legs and is also surrounded by long thick hairs. When the bee visits a flower, the pollen sticks to the thick hairs. While flying, the pollen dust is stripped off by the hairs of the rear legs, and with the help of the spurs on the legs the pollen is brushed from the comb into the basket.

While collecting the pollen, the bee fertilizes the flowers; the male particles of the pollen reach the

stigma and from there move through to the ovary; only then can seeds or fruit develop. Without this fertilization by bees, many of our native plants would bear no — or only meagre — fruit.

## Beehives

Stump beehives and skeps (wicker beehives) are among the oldest types of beehive. The stump hive is a hollow tree trunk, open at the bottom, with a flight opening (see next page). These days, beekeepers use wooden frames in trough and magazine hives, which are usually made of wood (see p. 90). With today's hives it's easier for the beekeeper to capture a swarm (see p. 89) as well as to multiply the colonies and care for each colony.

This type of stump beehive and the one below left can still be found today in Lithuania

◄
◄ Two stump beehives — the upper one
is a particularly funny example

Skeps were shaped like bells and made of braided willow branches or coiled straw, and caked with a mixture of clay and straw

*Straw hives were typical in the Rhineland in Germany up to about 1900*

# Bee Products

## ⊸ Honey

Honey is the most popular product of the beehive. It was mentioned in the Old Testament along with mead and olives as a reward in the Promised Land. It is the oldest sweetener in the world and still an important ingredient in old recipes. In modern cuisine it has more and more fans among health-conscious diners. It's most nutritious when eaten raw and cold; the substances in honey are sensitive to heat and so lose some of their nutritional value when cooked or baked.

## ⊸ Pollen

Pollen is also known as "flower dust;" the flowers are fertilized with pollen. Pollen is an important source of protein for bees, both for feeding larvae and bringing them to maturity. The insects collect pollen in clumps and form the clumps, with honey, into "bee bread" in the honeycombs.

## ⊸ Royal jelly

Royal jelly is the food of the queen bee; it is secreted by the female workers who produce it in modified salivary glands in their heads between their third and eleventh days. All bee larvae are fed this for three days. Workers and drones are then given honey and pollen; only the queen bee receives royal jelly for her entire life.

## ⊸ Propolis

Propolis is a resinous, aromatic material that bees collect from the buds of trees. The plants use this to protect their buds from drying out and from being attacked by parasites. The bees mix propolis with pollen, wax and saliva to produce a cement, which is then used to seal the cracks and seams of the hive. Even a flight hole that is too big can be reduced in size with propolis. Propolis kills germs and prevents disease in a bee colony. Enemies who have forced their way into the hive are killed and mummified with propolis.

## ⊸ Bee venom

Bee venom has been used for centuries to treat rheumatic illnesses. Remember that bees are naturally peaceful creatures; on the whole, their sting is to fight enemies of the same species.

## ⊸ Beeswax

The insects produce beeswax from their own body fat in the wax glands between their abdominal scales. Bees between twelve and eighteen days old secrete the colourless wax platelets and use them to construct the honeycombs. Every bee retains its functioning wax glands for its whole life.

Honeycombs serve as space for raising the brood and as storage space for pollen and honey. Honey and feeding cells are tightly sealed, while the brood cell coverings have holes that let air through for the developing bee.

Various factors are important for the building activity of a bee colony: available space, outside temperatures, food supply, and availability of nectar- and pollen-bearing plants. Extensive knowledge about the life of bees means the experienced beekeeper can appropriately support and nurture the hives.

Despite their impressive stability and load-bearing capacity, honeycombs are actually very light in weight. Humans have adopted honeycomb construction principles for use in airplanes and space capsules.

Through their work, beekeepers and bees contribute significantly to the ecological balance among native plants and animals. By their intensive pollination work, bees also contribute to the continuing diversity of plant species. This is essential to ensure the food supply for many living things.

*Rita Binz, a museum teacher*

## *Swarming*

Swarming is a phenomenon unique to honeybees. If the living space in a hive becomes too crowded, a new queen is bred, which stays with part of the colony, while the old queen swarms out with the larger part of the colony to find and establish a new territory.

*A beehive made by human hands consists of many individual parts that must all be cleaned carefully before a new colony can move in*

*After three days of quiet in the cellar, the captured swarm is carried to its new beehive at dawn*

*A curtain is used to secure the swarming hive. After it is removed, the bee colony will be moved into its new hive by gentle tapping.*

First, the entire colony hangs on a branch, looking like a fat bunch of grapes, to establish the community and be sure that the queen is unharmed in their midst. Now the beekeeper can capture the bee colony with a "swarming hive" (see above). He holds the hive with the opening pointing upward under the bunch of bees, and raps sharply on the branch that is holding the colony. The bunch loosens and falls into the hive. Bees remaining on the branch are removed gently with a goose feather, so that they are not separated from their colony (and especially from their queen). Then the hive is covered with a piece of loosely woven cloth (see above) and set onto a screen frame, so that air can circulate below.

A captured bee swarm is placed in a dark cool cellar for three days and three nights. Before swarming, the bees have stored adequate nourishment which they eat while in the cellar. The colony quiets down and loses its former orientation. It is then well prepared to be moved and settled into a new beehive at dawn.

## How Can Children Be Included in Beekeeping?

In the Children's Nature and Garden Centre, as mentioned above, we've had very positive experiences of involving children in beekeeping. Having said that, children should stand well back for all inspection and care tasks, except the treatment of varroa with acetic acid, and they should never stand in the way of key flight paths. It is important for humans:

* to approach the bees with inward and outward calm;

* not to cover themselves with too much perfume or toiletry fragrance;

* to respect the bee colony as a special social organism within the animal world.

*The bees take over their new hive very quickly, move into the honeycomb passageways between the wooden frames, and begin to establish their home. It's quite incredible: each bee knows immediately what must be done. Their greatest concern is the well-being of the queen.*

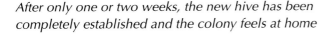

*After only one or two weeks, the new hive has been completely established and the colony feels at home*

Children intuitively imitate the behavior of adult companions, so it's important for teachers to have some basic knowledge of bees. Here are some suggestions:

✿ Adults are sometimes afraid of bees, but if they can overcome their fear, a wonderful world will open up for them when they accompany children to watch the beekeeper. The only reason not to participate in this is a serious *bee venom allergy,* which is rare (but check with your doctor).

✿ Every beekeeper knows his colonies so well that he can distinguish between non-stinging bees, which are friendly towards children, and stinging bees, which should be avoided. It is human beings themselves who, through their respectful and careful approach to the bees, partially determine the bees' behaviour.

✿ We always give some warning when we're visiting our colonies in the Children's Nature and Garden Centre. We sound an "A" tone with a tuning-fork, hold it onto the wooden

❀ Children should not be present when the honeycombs are removed, because the bees could become defensive. However, little sweet-toothed people are delighted to be around when the honey is centrifuged. They especially like to turn the handle of the honey extractor when the sweet, fragrant liquid gold flies out in viscous, amber-coloured threads from the honeycombs toward the walls of the centrifuge.

❀ One more suggestion is that schools and kindergartens which do keep animals, such as bees, for teaching purposes, should make this known in their literature and brochures for parents. Hopefully, it will encourage parents to enroll their child.

beehive as a resonating chamber, and thus signal to the six-legged inhabitants that we are coming. They're used to our careful and gentle approach, and so don't become aggressive. We give them water; we expand their living space; and in return we take some of their stored honey. They inherently know that their stored honey serves as nourishment for other living beings too, which is why they produce more than they need. In fact, if some were not removed, their living space would get very crowded.

# Further Reading

## – General

Freya Jaffke, *Work and Play in Early Childhood*, Anthroposophic Press, New York & Floris Books, Edinburgh.

Sally Jenkinson, *The Genius of Play*, Hawthorn Press, Stroud.

Martin Large, *Set Free Childhood*, Hawthorn Press, Stroud.

Nancy Mellon, *Storytelling with Children*, Hawthorn Press, Stroud.

Rudolf Meyer, *The Wisdom of Fairy Tales*, Floris Books, Edinburgh.

Lynne Oldfield, *Free to Learn*, Hawthorn Press, Stroud.

## – Crafts and activities

Joan Almon, *First Steps in Natural Dyeing*, Waldorf Kindergarten Assn. of North America.

Thomas & Petra Berger, *Crafts through the Year*, Floris Books, Edinburgh.

—, *The Gnome Craft Book*, Floris Books, Edinburgh.

Betsy Blumenthal and Kathryn Kreider, *Hands On Dyeing*, Interweave Press.

Rita Buchanan, *A Dyer's Garden: From Plant to Pot, Growing Dyes for Natural Fibers*, Interweave Press.

Christel Dhom, *Making Magical Fairy-tale Puppets*, Rudolf Steiner College Press, Fair Oaks.

Frieda Gates, *Johnny Appleseed: Fact and Fable*, Mercury Press.

M. van Leeuwen & J. Moeskops, *The Nature Corner*, Floris Books, Edinburgh.

Carol Petrash, *Earthways*, Gryphon House (published in UK as *Earthwise*, Floris Books, Edinburgh).

Dagmar Schmidt & Freya Jaffke, *Magic Wool*, Floris Books, Edinburgh.

Winston's Wish, *Muddles, Puddles and Sunshine*, Hawthorn Press, Stroud.

Angelika Wolk-Gerche, *More Magic Wool*, Floris Books, Edinburgh.

—, *Making Fairy-tale Wool Animals*, Rudolf Steiner College Press, Fair Oaks.

## – Songs and poems

Reeve Lindbergh (ed.), *In Every Tiny Grain of Sand*, Walker Books, London

Brien Masters (ed.), *The Waldorf Song Book*, Floris Books, Edinburgh.

Ann Pilling, *Before I go to Sleep*, Kingfisher Books, London.

Marlys Swinger (ed.), *Sing through the Day*, Plough Publishing House, New York & Sussex.

Marlys Swinger (ed.), *Sing through the Seasons*, Plough Publishing House, New York & Sussex.

## – Stories

Cicely Mary Barker, *Flower Fairies of the Spring*. Penguin.

Jean Giono, *The Man Who Planted Trees*. Boston: Shambhala Publications.

Reg Down, *The Tales of Tiptoes Lightly*. Trafford Publishing.

Jakob Streit, *Animal Stories*, Walter Keller Press, Dornach.

*The Complete Grimm's Tales for Young and Old*, Doubleday, New York, and Gollancz, London.

*Favourite Grimm's Tales*, illustrated by Anastasiya Archipova, Floris Books, Edinburgh.

Günther Hauck, *Towards Saving the Honeybee*, Biodynamic Farming & Gardening Ass. USA.

Nancy Jewel Poer, *Mia's Apple Tree*. White Feather Publishing Co.

*Spring* (songs and poems), Wynstones press.

## ～ Picture books

Elsa Beskow, *Around the Year,* Floris Books, Edinburgh.
Daniela Drescher, *In the Land of Fairies,* Floris Books, Edinburgh.
—, *In the Land of Elves,* Floris Books, Edinburgh.
Gerda Muller, *Spring* (a board book), Floris Books, Edinburgh.

## Sources for Natural Dyes

AUSTRALIA

Batik Oetoro, 203 Avoca Street, Randwick, NSW 2031. P.O. Box 324, Coogee, NSW 2034. Tel: 02-9398 6201, Fax: 02-9398 1173.

USA

— Alliance Import Co. 1021 "R" St., Sacramento, CA 95814 (large amounts, wholesale).
— Brooks & Flynn, Box 250, Rohnert Park, CA 94927.
— Cerulean Blue, Ltd., P.O. Box 21168, Seattle, WA 98111.
— Earth Guild, One Tingle Alley, Asheville, NC 28801.
— Ruppert, Gibbon and Spider, 718 College St., Healdsburg, CA 95448.

UK

P&M Woolcraft, Ashill Colour Studio, Pindon End, Hanslope, Milton Keynes, MK19 7HN. Tel: 01908 510277.

Fibrecrafts & George Weil, Old Portsmouth Road, Peasmarsh, Guildford, GU3 1LZ Tel: 01483 565 800, Fax: 01483 565 807. sales@georgeweil.co.uk

## Waldorf Schools

In June 2005 there were almost 900 Waldorf schools and 1,500 kindergartens in over 60 countries around the world. Up-to-date information can be found on any of the websites below.

Contact addresses in English-speaking countries:

AUSTRALIA

Association of Rudolf Steiner Schools in Australia, PO Box 111, Robertson, NSW 2577. rssa@bigpond.com, www.steineroz.com

NEW ZEALAND

Federation of Rudolf Steiner Schools, PO Box 888, Hastings, Hawkes Bay. waldorf@voyager.nz www.federation.steiner.school.nz

NORTH AMERICA

Association of Waldorf Schools of North America, 3911 Bannister Road, Fair Oaks, CA 95628. awsna@awsna.org, ww.waldorfeducation.org

SOUTH AFRICA

Southern African Federation of Waldorf Schools, PO Box 280, Plumstead 7801. federation@waldorf.org.za, www.waldorf.org.za

UK

Steiner Schools Fellowship, Kidbrooke Park, Forest Row, RH18 5JB. mail@swsf.org.uk, www.steinerwaldorf.org.uk

## Biodynamic Associations

AUSTRALIA

Biodynamic Agricultural Association, PO Box 54,
 Bellingen, NSW 2454.
Tel: 02-6655 0566, Fax: 02-6655 0565.
bdoffice@biodynamics.net.au
www.biodynamics.net.au

CANADA

Demeter Canada, 115 Des Myriques, Catevale Que.
 J0B 1W0.
Tel: 819-843-8488.
laurier.chabot@sympatico.ca
www.demetercanada.com

IRELAND

Biodynamic Agricultural Association,
 The Watergarden, Thomastown, Co. Kilkenny.
Tel/Fax: 56-54214.
bdaai@indigo.ie, www.demeter.ie

NEW ZEALAND

Biodynamic Farming & Gardening Association, PO
 Box 39045, Wellington Mail Centre.
Tel: 04-589 5366, Fax: 04-589 5365.
biodynamics@clear.net.nz, www.biodynamic.org.nz

SOUTH AFRICA

Biodynamic and Organic Agricultural Association,
 PO Box 115, 2056 Paulshof.
Tel: 011-803 1688,  Fax: 011-803 7191.

UK

Biodynamic Agricultural Association (BDAA),
 Painswick Inn, Gloucester Street, Stroud GL5 1QG.
Tel/Fax:01453 759501.
office@biodynamic.org.uk, www.biodynamic.org.uk

Myriad Natural Toys
43 Southampton Building
Ringwood BH24 1HE.
www.myriadonline.co.uk

USA

Biodynamic Farming and Gardening Association,
 25844 Butler Road, Junction City, OR 97448.
Tel: 888-516-7797 or 541-998-0105.
Fax: 541-998-0106.
biodynamic@aol.com, www.biodynamics.com

## The Children's Nature and Garden Centre

The Children's Nature and Garden Centre in Reichshof is open to all and offers seasonal nature classes. The Centre works closely with kindergartens and schools, and with parents. Its grounds are well equipped for practical, hands-on workshops, seminars and extended courses, and it also offers advice and support for those who want to set up similar schemes elsewhere.

For more information, contact the Centre at:

Natur-Kinder-Garten-Werkstatt Reichshof
Dorner Weg 4
51580 Reichshof
Germany

Tel.: +49-22 61-52 22 1
irmgardkutsch@aol.com

## Photograph and Illustration Credits

Fritz Hilgenstock: p. 55 (I)
Marcel Kalberer: p. 55 (II–V)
Erika Salaw: p. 75
Christian Tangemann: p. 54 (III), 86 (II, III), 89 (I, II), 90 (I)
Brigitte Walden: p. 50 (I)
Anke Wilhelm: p. 25 (I, II), 26, 27 (I–III), 28 (I, II), 37, 50 (III), 59 (I, III), 60 (I–III), 64, 81 (II, III)

All other photographs by Irmgard Kutsch

Archive for Art and History, Berlin: p. 15
Edgar Bayer: pp. 16, 43 (I, III), 44 (I-3), 52 (I,II), 60 (IV), 66
Christoph Buchen: p. 49
Marianne Frielingsdorf: p. 56
NUA/NRW: pp. 23, 24
Star Calendar Easter 1994/5, Verlag am Goetheanum, Dornach (changed), p. 14
Anke Wilhelm: 26, 32f, 42, 43 (II, IV, V), 53, 57, 58
Carolin Winkendick: p. 84